Samson

Man of strength, man of weakness

People IN THE BIBLE

Colin D Jones

DayOne

© Day One Publications 2007
First printed 2007

ISBN 978–1–84625–089–7

Unless otherwise stated, all Scripture quotations are from the
New International Version copyright © 1973, 1978, 1984

British Library Cataloguing in Publication Data available

Published by Day One Publications
Ryelands Road, Leominster, HR6 8NZ
☎ 01568 613 740 FAX 01568 611 473
email—sales@dayone.co.uk
web site—www.dayone.co.uk
North American—e-mail—sales@dayonebookstore.com
North American—web site—www.dayonebookstore.com

Cover design by Wayne McMaster
Designed by Steve Devane and printed by Gutenberg Press, Malta

Commendations

Samson is a man of many contrasts: a strong man, yet a weak man; a far-sighted yet a blind man; a spiritual man who is nevertheless a great sinner. So many contrasts, yet the most important opinion about Samson is that given to us in Hebrews 11—he is a great man of faith.

These contrasts are revealed in Colin D Jones' perceptive book, where Samson's life is also contrasted with that of the Lord Jesus, the true Judge who has liberated his people for ever.

Read this work for profit and praise, for a greater than Samson has come into the world.

—Clive Anderson, Pastor of 'The Butts' Church, Alton, Hampshire, England

Colin Jones has made an enigmatic narrative powerfully relevant. This is the story of Samson—for today. Careful exegesis, confronting the hard parts with honesty, and comparing and contrasting with the life of Jesus Christ, together with practical application, makes this commentary a powerful blend of personal Bible Study aid, a group discussion starter and a challenge for every Christian life. An accessible must for anyone interested in the life and times of Samson and its relevance for today.

—Brian H Edwards

Dedication

To my wife, Chris, my four daughters,

Esther, Abigail, Tirzah and Miriam,

and those 'encouragers in the congregation'.

It was your enthusiasm and persistence

that persuaded me to write at all.

Contents

Setting the scene

Before reading any further in this book, please take the time to read Judges 13–16. You might find it helpful to read it in several different translations to fix the flow of the story in your mind. It will not take you long and the time spent will be well rewarded. No book about the Word of God can ever replace reading the Scriptures themselves.

A mixture of a man

The opening words of Judges 13 serve as a summary of the entire narrative and provide the necessary backdrop to an understanding of Samson the man. They are both a searchlight on the frailty of mankind and an incredible commentary on the astounding mercy and grace of God. Throughout Judges we see a nation in perpetual failure and sin being met by a God of both justice and mercy. In Samson we will see a man of faith (Hebrews 11:32), yes, but also a man of great personal weakness. He steps out of the pages of Scripture with a stunning modernity. He is like one of the great 'heroes' of our 21st-century culture, reminding us of a sportsman or movie star who thrills us on the field or screen but is revealed in the tabloids as deeply flawed and often sadly isolated.

Samson is such a man; none can fail to thrill at his incredible feats of strength accomplished by the power of God's Spirit. Yet scrutiny of his private life reveals a weak, self-indulgent man, given to fits of rage; a morally weak man fatally attracted to the wrong women. He is a lonely man, seemingly without friends or companions, ploughing his solitary furrow towards self-destruction. Paradoxically, it is only at the end when he is rendered physically weak that he exhibits real strength; only when blinded by his enemies does he truly see himself, his mission and his God.

As we study this remarkable man we will learn much about our own culture, our own weaknesses and, above all, much about the God of grace who despite all the failings of his servant still used him to accomplish his divine purposes. We will see what God did through Samson and despite Samson, and marvel again at the contrast with God's one 'perfect servant', the God-man Jesus Christ.

A familiar lament (13:1)

'*Again* the Israelites did evil in the eyes of the LORD, *so* the LORD delivered them into the hands of the Philistines for forty years' (emphasis mine). Let's focus for just a moment on two words in this first verse.

AGAIN

The use of this word reminds us that God is constantly dealing with a fallen creation that has a bias towards sin. Émile Coué, the French psychotherapist (1857–1926),[1] could not have been more wrong when he said that 'every day in every way we are getting better and better'. In reality we have all 'sinned and fallen short of the glory of God' (Romans 3:23). The sinful life of Samson is not an isolated occurrence in the history of the nation, nor is he a uniquely sinful individual: sadly this is the norm, not the exception. The Bible reveals that:

- We are sinners by *choice*—countless times throughout our lives we reaffirm Adam's rebellion (Genesis 3), defying God and choosing our own way.
- We are sinners by *habit*—each wrong choice making it more likely that we will sin again.
- We are sinners by *neglect*—failing time and again to do that which is right and within our power to do (James 4:17).

SO

Sin is never without consequences. The consequence for Israel in this portion of Judges was forty years of oppression by the Philistines.[2] The consequence for Samson was eventual capture, humiliation, torture and blindness. The consequence for us as individuals, unless we seek the forgiveness and cleansing offered only through Jesus Christ (Acts 4:12), is certain death followed by equally certain judgement (Romans 6:23).

A familiar situation (13:2)

'A certain man of Zorah, named Manoah, from the clan of the Danites, had a wife who was sterile and remained childless.' It is interesting to note how often remarkable characters in the Scripture are introduced to us through special birth narratives. Samson finds himself in exalted company here. Barrenness is often, though not always, the precursor in such accounts:

- Barren Sarah eventually gives birth to Isaac and becomes the mother of the Hebrew nation (Genesis 16–21).
- Barren Hannah gives birth to Samuel, the last of the judges and (with the exception of Moses) the first great prophet (1 Samuel 1:1–20).
- Barren Elizabeth becomes the mother of John the Baptist. John is destined to be the last of that great line of Old Testament prophets, and the forerunner of Jesus Christ (Luke 1).
- Mary the mother of Jesus was, of course, not barren but her miraculous conceiving through the agency of the Holy Spirit in place of any human father must be included in this list—the fruit of that miracle being none other than the Lord Jesus Christ himself.

The first and the last of our list, Sarah and Mary, form a bridge to another remarkable and noteworthy feature of Samson's birth—that of angelic announcement. Clearly this is to be no ordinary child.

A familiar truth (13:4)

'Now see to it that you drink no wine or other fermented drink and that you do not eat anything unclean.'

Though, as we have remarked, the life of Samson was sadly lacking in holiness, holiness remains a requirement of the holy God, especially for his chosen people. This is expressed here, as in much of the Old Testament, in terms of ceremonial cleanness. Samson is to be a Nazirite from his birth. Nazirites were widespread among ancient peoples, taking the common vows of abstinence from alcohol, avoidance of dead bodies, and allowing the hair to grow uncut. It was supposed to signify a special degree of dedication and personal holiness. We will look at these vows in more detail in the next chapter. As the narrative unfolds we will see that Samson breaks this vow and consequently falls short of his high calling.

A familiar confusion (13:6)

'Then the woman went to her husband and told him, "A man of God came to me. He looked like an angel of God, very awesome. I didn't ask him where he came from, and he didn't tell me his name."'

As we come to this verse we must ask ourselves the question—Is this a theophany?[3] 'Theophany' is the term given to those appearances in the Old Testament of a being known as 'the angel of the LORD'. Elwell comments:

In certain texts, it seems impossible to distinguish between the angel of the Lord and the Lord himself (Genesis 16:7–13; 21:17; 22:11–18; 24:7,40; 31:11–13; 48:16; Exodus 3:2–10; Judges 6:12–14; 13:21–22). Sometimes the angel is depicted acting for the Lord and yet is addressed as the Lord.

The angel seems to possess the full authority and character of God. The presence of the messenger of the Lord, in whom God's 'name' resides (Exodus 23:20) assures the hearer-reader that it is one God who directs the course of history (Genesis 16:7; 31:11; Exodus 3:2).[4]

It is most probable that these are appearances of God the Son in human history prior to the incarnation. Though it was not until the incarnation that Jesus took upon himself human flesh, on these earlier occasions he 'appeared' as a man. Appearing as men is something that the angels of God also do on occasion—compare, for instance, the resurrection account by Matthew with those by Mark and Luke (Matthew 28:1–8; Mark 16:1–8; and Luke 24:1–10). Matthew speaks of an angel while the others refer to men. This is not an inconsistency: Mark and Luke are telling us what they saw; Matthew goes behind the perception to the reality.

My heading for this section is not intended to suggest that encounters with God in this way are 'familiar' in the sense that they are a common occurrence: clearly they are rare. Rather, my point is that any encounter with God, through creation, providence, Scripture, preaching or any other means, frequently produces similar results.

With these encounters there is often an initial uncertainty as to who we are encountering and the significance of the encounter (Judges 13:6, 16). The Ethiopian eunuch (Acts 8:34), Saul of Tarsus (Acts 9:5) and the people of Lystra (Acts 14:8–18) all exhibited the same confusion we see in Manoah and his wife.

As revelation increases there is an enhanced desire to remain in the presence of God (Judges 13:15). We see this with Moses (Exodus 33:12–

16), Peter, James and John (Matthew 17:4), and in the disciples' consternation at the news that Jesus was departing from them (John 14).

Next there comes a genuine desire to know more about God (Judges 13:17). This is exemplified in Luke's pen-portrait of the early church living in a community based around prayer and the study of the Word of God (Acts 2:42–47).

A feature of encounters with God that seems common in Scripture, but is sadly much rarer today, is that of fear. That fear is generated by an awareness of God's holiness and our own personal sin, often resulting in a state of near despair. We see it in Isaiah (Isaiah 6:5), Peter (Luke 5:8) and many others.

This is no groundless fear; it compels us to consider the subjects of death and judgement as stark realities. Man without Christ has much to fear: he is doomed to an unfulfilled searching and an unsatisfied yearning. He will not find satisfaction in wealth, fame, knowledge, achievement, sex or personal relationships. Man was made for God and only God can fully satisfy him.

A familiar comfort (13:22)

'"We are doomed to die!" he said to his wife. "We have seen God!"'

The command 'Do not be afraid' is at the heart of the gospel. Often it is direct from the mouth of God (Luke 1:13,30; 2:10; 5:10; 8:50; 12:4,7,32; Hebrews 13:6; Revelation 2:10; and many other verses). Here Manoah's wife uses her God-given logic to deduce peace and comfort from the character of God and his actions towards them. She rightly reasons that God would not have revealed himself and his message to them unless he meant it for their good.

We are justified in using a similar 'logic':
• Would God have spared mankind unless he purposed good for us?
• Would he have spoken to us through his Word?
• Would he have warned us about sin and encouraged us towards holiness?
• Would he have given us his law?
• Would he have given us his prophets?
• Would he have given us his Son?

- Would he have spoken to us through his Scriptures?
- Would he have spoken to us through his preachers?
- Would he have offered us salvation if it was not his desire to give it?

Proverbs 9:10 rightly argues that 'the fear of the LORD is the beginning of wisdom, and knowledge of the Holy One is understanding.'

The wise man or woman will deduce from all these things that God is to be found by those who seek him (Matthew 7:7).

The person of Christ

One must wholeheartedly agree with Gordon Keddie when he says that 'Samson's life is not an allegory about Jesus—as Bunyan's *Pilgrim's Progress* is an allegory about the Christian life'.5 There are, however, always lessons to be learnt about the Saviour from every portion of Scripture. The Bible from Genesis to Revelation is about Christ. In some aspects there can be no greater contrast than that between Samson and Christ. Moral failure is set against absolute purity, destructive force against a ministry of healing and gentleness. There are, however, points of similarity: both are judges (2 Corinthians 5:10; 2 Timothy 4:1; Jude 14–15) and both deliverers (Romans 11:26)—though in Samson's case the delivery was only partial (13:5) while that of Christ is perfectly complete. They each manifest strength but in very different ways: Samson's is a violent, physical form; Christ's the ultimate manifestation of submission to the commandments of God.

In setting the scene for Samson we are, of course, verging on a much wider discussion, that of the coming of Christ. The problems that beset Samson are to an extent present in all humankind. Each of the Bible heroes is portrayed in the manner insisted on by the Lord Protector Oliver Cromwell when admonishing his portrait painter: 'Remark all these roughnesses, pimples, warts, and everything as you see me, otherwise I will never pay a farthing for it.'6 The whole of history is one unending search for the perfect man, the perfect deliverer, a search that ends only when John the Baptist proclaims, 'Look, the Lamb of God, who takes away the sin of the world!' (John 1:29) It is fitting that when Christ entered the world it was not merely to the announcement of one angel but to the sung praises of an innumerable host (Luke 2:8–14). Still there was the need for the encouragement: 'Do not be afraid. I bring you good news of great joy that will be for all the people' (Luke 2:10). Until Christ's redemptive work at Calvary was completed there could be no blanket assurance expressed by his people as we find in Hebrews 10:19–22:

Therefore, brothers, since we have confidence to enter the Most Holy Place by the blood of Jesus, by a new and living way opened for us through the curtain, that is, his body, and since we have a great priest over the house of God, let us draw near to God with a sincere heart in full assurance of faith, having our hearts sprinkled to cleanse us from a guilty conscience and having our bodies washed with pure water.

Questions

COMPARING SCRIPTURE WITH SCRIPTURE

1. The Samson story is an alliteration-loving preacher's delight. Consider the four Rs: Rebellion, Retribution, Repentance and Restoration. To what extent is Judges in general and Samson in particular a picture of the entire history of mankind and a clear gospel outline?

2. Why do men not immediately recognize the revelation or presence of God? (See John 12:37–41; 2 Corinthians 4:2–6; Ephesians 4:18–20; Romans 1.)

3. What can and should be done about this situation? (See Hebrews 3:8–15; Romans 10:9.)

APPLYING SCRIPTURE TO DAILY LIFE

1. Revisit the four Rs (Rebellion, Retribution, Repentance and Restoration) and consider how they apply to personal, church and national life.

2. Samson demonstrates that a person can be blessed by God despite his or her personal sins. What comfort can we draw from this? (See Jonah 3:1; Mark 16:7; 1 Timothy 1:12–17.) What dangers does it open up? (See Proverbs 1:32; Romans 6:1; Jeremiah 7:1–8.)

3. Why and when should an initial fear of God give way to joy and pleasure in his presence? What brings about such a dramatic change?

Notes

1 http://www.quotationspage.com/quotes/Emile_Coue/ [accessed 27 June 2006].

2 See Appendix.

3 For a detailed treatment of this subject see **Jonathan Stephen's** excellent book *Theophany* (Epsom: Day One Publications, 1998).

4 **W. A. Elwell and P. W. Comfort,** *Tyndale Bible Dictionary*, Vol. 1, Tyndale Reference Library (Wheaton, IL: Tyndale House Publishers, 2001), p. 90.

5 **G. Keddie,** *Even in Darkness*, Welwyn Commentary Series (Welwyn: Evangelical Press), 1985, p. 97.

6 http://en.thinkexist.com/quotation/remark_all_these_roughnesses-pimples-warts-and/262141.html [accessed 28 June 2006].

The Nazirite vow

The Hebrew word translated Nazirite, *nāzîr*, has the literal meaning of 'consecrated' or 'devoted one'; it comes from *nāzar*, 'to consecrate' or 'separate [oneself]'.[1] It also has the meaning 'a diadem', the 'crown of God', possibly derived from the Nazirite's uncut hair.[2] The prohibitions of the vow (see below) may have been linked with the worst features of Canaanite worship. Certainly that relating to alcohol evidences a wider biblical concern. This is reflected in the restriction imposed on the priesthood: 'Then the LORD said to Aaron, "You and your sons are not to drink wine or other fermented drink whenever you go into the Tent of Meeting, or you will die. This is a lasting ordinance for the generations to come"' (Leviticus 10:8–9).

We also see it in the general warning of Proverbs: 'Wine is a mocker and beer a brawler; whoever is led astray by them is not wise' (20:1); and in the sad example of Noah: 'Noah, a man of the soil, proceeded to plant a vineyard. When he drank some of its wine, he became drunk and lay uncovered inside his tent' (Genesis 9:20–21).

Amos links the corruption of the Nazirites along with the silencing of the prophets as one of the chief causes of the apostasy that characterized his own day:

'I also raised up prophets from among your sons
    and Nazirites from among your young men.
Is this not true, people of Israel?' declares the LORD.
'But you made the Nazirites drink wine
    and commanded the prophets not to prophesy' (Amos 2:11–12).

The prophet Samuel may well have been a Nazirite[3]—certainly the vow relating to the cutting of hair was applied to him (1 Samuel 1:11).

In order to understand Samson and his Nazirite vow it is important to read Numbers 6:1–21 carefully. The most important aspects as they affect the life of Samson are outlined below:
• 'He must abstain from wine and other fermented drink … As long as he is a Nazirite … (6:3–4).

- 'During the entire period of his vow of separation no razor may be used on his head. ... He must let the hair of his head grow long' (6:5).
- 'Throughout the period of his separation to the Lord he must not go near a dead body' (6:6).

The significance of these three aspects is heightened in Samson's case because his status as a Nazirite was to be in force throughout his life. He was dedicated at the moment of conception and only death could release him from it. Consequently there are two ways of understanding the sin of Samson and his subsequent loss of strength.

According to the first understanding Samson progressively breaks all three aspects of the vow, and when the final transgression is made, forfeits his strength from God. If we follow this line of reasoning then the first transgression is recorded in 14:8–9, when he scoops the honey from the carcass of the lion he has slain. This interpretation requires an understanding of 'dead body' in Numbers 6:6 to refer to any cadaver, not just a human one. It seems far from certain that the text should be stretched to accommodate such an understanding. A second assumption is also needed to sustain this first theory and that is in connection with the prohibition on alcohol. Samson's wedding reception was, as we will see later, set against the backdrop of a drinking bout. The text does not, however, say that Samson himself partook of the alcohol that would have been available in plentiful supply. Equally, it seems unwarranted to argue that 'A vineyard was a dangerous place for a man who was not supposed to have anything to do with grapes', which is the point Warren Wiersbe makes in relation to Samson's journey recorded in 14:5.4 Neither of these incidents seems conclusively to point to a break in the vow and, most significantly, Scripture nowhere designates them as such.

The simpler explanation seems the best: that the breaking of the vow was solely accomplished through the cutting of his hair.

The person of Christ

Professor John G. Gammie agues that: 'In the NT it is likely that one of the significances attached to Jesus' being called a "Nazarene" (Matthew 2:23) is that he too should be viewed as a Nazirite in the sense of being consecrated to God from the womb.'5

This idea, though popular, is fraught with difficulty. Jesus certainly did not avoid dead bodies; indeed there are a number of occasions when he is specifically recorded as being in close proximity to them. In the account of the miracle of the raising of Jairus' daughter we are expressly told that 'he took her by the hand' before raising her to life again (Mark 5:22–43).

There are further difficulties when we come to the question of alcohol. Jesus' first miracle was, after all, the changing of water into wine (John 2). He was accused of being a drunkard: 'The Son of Man came eating and drinking, and they say, "Here is a glutton and a drunkard, a friend of tax collectors and 'sinners'." But wisdom is proved right by her actions' (Matthew 11:19); however, this was undoubtedly a gross exaggeration and distortion of the truth. We do know that he did indeed eat in the homes of tax collectors and sinners. We have no evidence either way on the issue of his drinking alcohol, in moderation, in their company.

It is also true of course that the New Testament furnishes us with no physical description of Jesus so the length of his hair is a matter of complete conjecture. We do know that the Apostle Paul said, 'If a man has long hair, it is a disgrace to him' (1 Corinthians 11:14). Though this was written in a Gentile context it seems highly unlikely that he would have made such a remark if the Lord himself had the flowing locks so familiar to us from the artist's brush.

That Jesus was a Nazirite, is, I feel, wholly unproven and extremely unlikely.

The consecration of the Saviour to his Father's will and purpose is, however, a totally different matter. While the obedience of Samson was found wanting, that of Jesus was total; while the life of Samson was flawed, that of Jesus was beyond reproach.

Dedication to God was the hallmark of Jesus' life from start to finish. As a child he questioned why his parents were perplexed and concerned over his whereabouts. In reply to their rebuke, when their frantic search finally located him in the temple precincts, he calmly asked, 'Why were you searching for me? … Didn't you know I had to be in my Father's house?' (Luke 2:49).

The writer to the Hebrews was inspired to place the words of Psalm

```
```

40:6–8 into the mouth of Jesus: 'Here I am—it is written about me in the scroll—I have come to do your will, O God' (Hebrews 10:7).

There was a holy determination evident towards the end of his earthly ministry when he told his disciples: 'We are going up to Jerusalem ... and the Son of Man will be betrayed to the chief priests and teachers of the law. They will condemn him to death and will hand him over to the Gentiles' (Mark 10:33).

There is a quiet dignity and profound resolve reflected in Luke's observation: 'As the time approached for him to be taken up to heaven, Jesus *resolutely* set out for Jerusalem' (Luke 9:51, emphasis mine). The KJV[6] renders the same verse: 'And it came to pass, when the time was come that he should be received up, *he steadfastly set his face* to go to Jerusalem' (emphasis mine).

Despite his complete awareness of all that lay before him, he was resolute in following the path his Father had ordained for him. Even in his darkest hour, in the Garden of Gethsemane, his horror of all that awaited him was overruled by his utter obedience to his divine mission: 'Going a little farther, he fell with his face to the ground and prayed, "My Father, if it is possible, may this cup be taken from me. Yet not as I will, but as you will"' (Matthew 26:39).

Questions

COMPARING SCRIPTURE WITH SCRIPTURE

1. Consider the story in 1 Samuel 15 particularly as it relates to the subject of obedience. Give special consideration to verses 22–23.

2. What are the characteristics of true obedience? (See Deuteronomy 11:13–14; Romans 6:17; Isaiah 1:19–20; Deuteronomy 28:14; Philippians 2:12–13.)

3. Why does Paul take what appears to be a vow, very similar to the Nazirite vow, in Acts 18:18?

APPLYING SCRIPTURE TO DAILY LIFE

1. What attitude towards vows should be generated by a study of Proverbs 20:25 and Ecclesiastes 5:4–7?

Chapter 2

2. What practical steps can we take to increase our obedience to God?
3. What would you consider to be a wise attitude towards the use of alcohol?

Notes

1 A. C. Myers, *The Eerdmans Bible Dictionary* (Grand Rapids, MI: Eerdmans, 1987), p. 751, and F. Brown, S. R. Driver and C. A. Briggs, *Enhanced Brown-Driver-Briggs Hebrew and English Lexicon* (electronic ed.) (Oak Harbor, WA: Logos Research Systems).

2 D. R. W. Wood, *New Bible Dictionary* (Leicester: InterVarsity Press, 1996), p. 808.

3 P. J. Achtemeier, ed., Harper & Row and Society of Biblical Literature, *Harper's Bible Dictionary* (San Francisco: Harper & Row, 1985), p. 690.

4 W. W. Wiersbe, *Be Available* (Wheaton, IL: Victor Books, 1996), p. 111.

5 John G. Gammie, in Achtemeier, Harper, Row and Society of Biblical Literature, *Harper's Bible Dictionary*, p. 690.

6 *The Holy Bible: King James Version*, 1995 (electronic edition of the Authorized Version, 1769).

Ups, downs and other devices

The full beauty and complexity of the Samson narratives is often lost on the casual reader and perhaps only fully yielded to those fortunate enough to study it in the original language. There is, however, much that we can see if we just look carefully.

The writer is a genius at storytelling. When I was a child I was occasionally permitted to join the queues outside our local cinema in South Wales for the Saturday treat known as the *ABC Minors*; though my visits were infrequent, they have left a clear and pleasant impression. I well remember singing the theme song:

We are the boys and girls well known
as Minors of the ABC
And every Saturday we line up
 To see the films we like
 And shout aloud with glee
We love to laugh and have a singsong
Such a happy crowd are we
We're all pals together
The minors of the ABC.[1]

But for me the greatest delight was not the singing but the serial story, which always ended in a 'cliff-hanger', the hero often, quite literally, hanging on the edge of doom and destruction. It was designed to create an overwhelming desire to return the next week to see what happened, and, I might add, it was successful in doing so.

The Samson story is written in much the same style. How is Samson's desire for the Timnite going to precipitate conflict with the Philistines (14:4)? Why are we told that the incident with the lion was kept secret from his parents (14:9)? What will happen when Samson reaches the Timnite's house and discovers she is married to another (14:20–15:1)? How will he escape from the hands of the men of Judah (15:11–12)? Will he die of thirst in the aftermath of his great exertions at Jawbone Hill (15:18)? Will the

Philistines lying in wait for him in Gaza capture him at dawn (16:1–2)? Will he find true love and happiness in the arms of Delilah (16:4)? Will her treachery finally lead to his downfall (16:5)? Will the growth of his hair mean the return of his strength (16:22)? And finally, and most compelling of all: Is our blind hero really finished or will God somehow come to his aid just one more time (16:25)? It takes little imagination to see how the story can be told in a way that would keep any child (or adult) on the edge of his or her seat waiting for the next instalment. Each 'cliff-hanger' advances the storyline and most are preludes to great acts of God.

We need also to take note of other literary devices the writer employs if we are to appreciate fully the wisdom with which he writes.

There are, for instance, plays on words, one of which we will comment on here and the others later, where they occur in the narrative. Kim says that the name Samson means 'little sun' or 'sunny' and argues that the choice of name 'clearly reflects the expectation of the parent that through this child a new dawning of freedom and salvation would come to Israel'.[2] If so, this was an expectation that would, at best, find only partial fulfilment.

Samson is set before us as an invincible warrior, yet we are constantly reminded that in the arms of a woman he is both weak and foolish. The riddle given in answer to that set by Samson (14:18) has an obvious solution: in the context of a wedding the answer is surely love—'stronger than a lion yet sweeter than honey'. The reverse, however, is true in Samson's case; love has made him both weak and bitter.

There is a play on the theme of light and darkness. Many of the scenes in the story are linked in some way to this theme. Samson lights up the sky with the fire set by the jackals (or foxes—15:4–5); his staying the night with the prostitute in Gaza endangers his life (16:1–3); it is while he sleeps that Delilah plots against him (16:14); and it is in the darkness brought about by the gouging-out of his eyes that he finally sees and triumphs (16:21–31).

Wilcock and others rightly see significance in the repeated use of the term 'down' in the narrative.[3] Samson goes 'down' to Timnah and sees the woman he wants for his wife (14:1). Later we are told three times that the direction travelled is 'down' as his parents journey with him to seal the marriage (14:5,7,10). He again goes 'down' to Ashkelon, to kill the thirty

Philistines and strip them of their belongings (14:19). It is 'down' to the cave at Etam that he goes after his vicious slaughter in revenge for his wife's death (15:8). The men of Judah have to come 'down' to him there to secure him as a captive and save their own lives (15:11). After the betrayal by Delilah it is 'down' to Gaza that the Philistines take him for torture and humiliation (16:21). Finally it is again 'down' that his whole family journeys to retrieve his body and give the burial a judge of Israel deserves (16:31). It is a literary device that helps hold the narrative together. It also serves to remind us of the constant failure of our hero to 'live up' to his calling as a judge in Israel.

The old children's hymn has the verse:

God has given us a book full of stories,
Which was made for his people of old.
It begins with the tale of a garden
And it ends with a City of Gold.4

The story of Samson is one of those excellent and brilliantly written stories. The first line of the next verse rightly says: 'But the best is the story of Jesus.'

The person of Christ

Even the writer of the Samson story pales into insignificance beside the Lord Jesus Christ. Believer and unbeliever alike are to some extent aware of his memorable teaching and teaching methods. In the West we seem to have lost the art of storytelling as an element in preaching. We have become narrowed down to the cerebral, reasoned argument that some would contend owes more to Greek culture than to the Bible. Please do not misunderstand me; I am not saying that there is no place for such preaching: there is. The magnificent letter of Paul to the Romans is a superb example of reasoned argument at its very best. No one, I trust, would argue that the gospel is not both fully and clearly explained in that wonderful letter. All I plead for is that we do not neglect the power of storytelling. Is the reason why many adults prefer the children's talk to the sermon only a reflection of shallowness and lack of spiritual appetite? May it not also be that those of us who are preachers have lost the art of amply lacing our sermons with memorable phrases and pertinent illustrations? Stuart Olyott devotes a whole chapter to what he calls 'vivid illustration' in his excellent book *Preaching pure and simple.5*

Consider for a moment some aspects of the teaching ministry of Jesus.

He sometimes based his teaching on well-known or current events; the eighteen who died in the collapse of the tower in Siloam becomes a vehicle for pressing the urgency of repentance (Luke 13:4); the visit of the deputation sent by John the Baptist from his prison cell is utilized to teach the nature of the kingdom of God (Matthew 11:1–19). On one occasion Jesus cried out with a loud voice: 'If anyone is thirsty, let him come to me and drink.' Don Carson gives us the background to this incident recorded in John 7:37:

On the seven days of the Feast, a golden flagon was filled with water from the pool of Siloam and was carried in a procession led by the High Priest back to the temple. As the procession approached the water gate on the south side of the inner court three blasts from the šôpār—a trumpet connected with joyful occasions—were sounded. While the pilgrims watched, the priests processed around the altar with the flagon, the temple choir singing the Hallel (Psalms 113–118).6

Against that background the claim of Jesus takes on a new and dramatic significance.

The stories that Jesus told, though recounted briefly in the Gospels, are enduringly memorable. The three stories of the lost—sheep, coin and son (Luke 15)—the tale of the good Samaritan (Luke 10:25–37) and many others are so skilfully constructed that once heard they are never forgotten.

Then there are the unforgettable pithy pictures and sayings about a camel passing through the eye of a needle (Matthew 19:23–24), or giving to Caesar what is Caesar's and to God what is God's (Mark 12:17).

The preaching ministry of Jesus was immensely powerful for a number of reasons: his teaching was from God not a mere man (John 14:24); it was delivered with divine authority (Matthew 7:29); it was rooted in Scripture (Mark 12:10); it was backed up with a godly life (John 10:37). Even with all of this in place the Lord ensured that it was also delivered in a way that was accessible and memorable. Surely all of these elements should be present in any and every sermon preached.

God has given us a revelation of himself in the Bible. It is an amazing book, full of history, poetry and law. There are sections of concise wisdom (Proverbs), but above all stories, stories, stories.

Questions

COMPARING SCRIPTURE WITH SCRIPTURE

1. Which Old Testament story do you find most interesting? What does it teach?

2. Make a list of what *you think* are the five most memorable stories Jesus told. What does each one teach?

3. Make a list of what *you think* are the five most memorable sayings of Jesus. What does each one teach?

APPLYING SCRIPTURE TO DAILY LIFE

1. In the tension between 'presentation' and 'content' in gospel preaching, which do you think is the most important and why? Do we give enough attention to presentation?

2. If you are a preacher, how could you improve your sermons? If you are not, how could you listen better?

Notes

1 http://www.seniorsnetwork.co.uk/reminiscence/abcminors.htm [accessed 14 August 2006].

2 **J. Kim,** *The Structure of the Samson Cycle* (Kampen, Netherlands: Kok Pharos Publishing House, 1993), p. 214.

3 **M. Wilcock,** *The Message of the Judges*, The Bible Speaks Today Series (Leicester: Inter-Varsity Press, 1992), p. 135.

4 **Maria Matilda Penstone** (1859–1910), no. 216 in *The School Hymnbook* of the Methodist Church.

5 **S. Olyott,** *Preaching Pure and Simple* (Bridgend: Bryntirion Press, 2005), p. 92.

6 **D. A. Carson,** *The Gospel According to John* (Leicester: Inter-Varsity Press, 1991), p. 321.

Samson's parents

A s we begin to read Judges 14 we have jumped, without comment, from Samson's birth to his manhood. We discover that he has journeyed from his home to the Philistine town of Timnah, where a young woman has caught his eye. Immediately we find ourselves asking questions about his attitude to his parents and to the one who is the first in what will become a long and sorry line of women.

The character of his parents

We noted briefly in the opening chapter something of the character of Samson's parents. We will look at them now in a little more detail. They occupy centre stage in chapter 13, become bit players in chapter 14 and are absent from the remainder of the narrative. His father, we are told, is called Manoah, but his mother remains unnamed. In chapter 13 we learn a number of pertinent facts about them both.

They seem, on the face of it, to be a good and godly couple. If they are somewhat lacking in spiritual maturity, it is a fault that might better be attributed to the general state of the nation than solely to them as individuals. They are Danites living in the town of Zorah and are enduring the sad state of childlessness.

The angelic visitor insists that prior to Samson's conception his mother must assume some of the obligations of a Nazirite vow and keep them for the remainder of her days. The proscription against using a razor is, however, reserved for her unborn son.

She recognizes the visitor as 'a man of God' (13:6) from his appearance and possibly from his message. Manoah, not present at this remarkable encounter, understandably seeks from God the blessing of another visitation. He is looking for further instruction on the upbringing of their 'miracle child'. It is worth noting that, while a second visitation is granted, God has nothing further to add to his previous commands. God always reveals all that is necessary for the implementation of his will. In this regard there is great reassurance to be had from the words of Jesus to his disciples in the upper room: 'In my Father's house are many rooms; *if it were not so,*

I would have told you. I am going there to prepare a place for you' (John 14:2, emphasis mine).

Manoah's natural desire is to prolong the spiritual experience and this finds an echo in the words of Peter on the Mount of Transfiguration: 'Peter said to Jesus, "Lord, it is good for us to be here. If you wish, I will put up three shelters—one for you, one for Moses and one for Elijah"' (Matthew 17:4).

We have already commented on the fear that a dawning awareness of the identity of their guest produces in Manoah, and on the wisdom his wife displays in calming those fears.

Samson's relationship with his parents

We are dependent on the small section in 14:2–10 for our source material on this subject. It is, however, more than sufficient to cause us to question Samson's obedience to the fifth commandment: 'Honour your father and your mother, so that you may live long in the land the LORD your God is giving you' (Exodus 20:12). It also seems likely that he forsook the blessing that was promised to the obedient. We are not told how old Samson was at his death, but as he judged Israel for only twenty years and was in vigorous (the Philistines would say, dangerous) health when he was captured, it seems certain that he did not die in old age.

His dealings with his father over the matter of his Timnite bride are, to say the least, curt. Manoah has genuine and well-grounded reasons for opposing the match as an unwise and unacceptable one. The threefold repetition in 14:1–3 that she is a Philistine reaches a climax with the adding of the pejorative 'uncircumcised' to the ethnic description lest the point be missed. This woman does not belong to the covenant people of God, nor is there any indication that unlike Ruth (Ruth 1:16–18) and Rahab (Joshua 2:7–15) she wishes to do so. The marriage is therefore illicit and Manoah's objection valid. Esau so grieved his father, with his marriage to a Canaanite woman, that Isaac explicitly forbad Jacob to follow suit (Genesis 28:6–8). Solomon was led into idolatry by making marriage alliances for reasons of state (1 Kings 11:4). Rather than listening or explaining, Samson sharply commands his father's compliance, thus reversing their God-ordained roles.

The second issue we must examine, as we seek to evaluate Samson the son, is connected with two aspects of the incident of the lion and the honey. Twice we are told that Samson neglected to tell his parents significant facts. His slaying of the lion is the first occasion of divine intervention in his life and the evidence that the promises made prior to his birth are beginning to be fulfilled ('The boy is to be a Nazirite, set apart to God from birth, and he will begin the deliverance of Israel from the hands of the Philistines', 13:5). It would not have been boasting on his part, rather a testimony to the grace of God to have related these events. Samson seems simply not to have bothered to tell the most interested parties—his own parents.

On the second occasion he fails to tell them the source of the honey and, in consequence, may have caused them, along with himself, to violate the law of God. In Leviticus we read the following:

- 'You will make yourselves unclean by these; whoever touches their carcasses will be unclean till evening' (11:24).
- 'Anyone, whether native-born or alien, who eats anything found dead or torn by wild animals must wash his clothes and bathe with water, and he will be ceremonially unclean till evening; then he will be clean' (17:15).
- And particularly: 'If a person touches anything ceremonially unclean—whether the carcasses of unclean wild animals or of unclean livestock or of unclean creatures that move along the ground—even though he is unaware of it, he has become unclean and is guilty' (5:2).

These prohibitions are germane to this situation: they seem to suggest that Samson, while not specifically breaking his Nazirite vow, may well have been defiling both himself and his parents by his actions.

The person of Christ

It will not surprise us in the least to discover that the perfect man, Jesus of Nazareth, lived his childhood as the perfect son. It has been well said that, if you want the truth about your faults, ask an enemy or a really good friend. We have the testimony of both concerning Jesus. When his enemies mustered their accusations the best they could come up with were misrepresentations of his plain teaching, such as we read in Matthew: 'The chief priests and the whole Sanhedrin were looking for false evidence against Jesus so that they could put him to death. But they did not find any, though many false witnesses came forward. Finally two came forward and declared, "This fellow said, 'I am able to destroy the temple of God and rebuild it in three days'"' (Matthew 26:59–61).

We also find an incredibly feeble attempt: 'The Son of Man came eating and drinking, and they say, "Here is a glutton and a drunkard, a friend of tax collectors and 'sinners'"' (Matthew 11:19). What else would be expected of one who had come 'to seek and save what was lost' (Luke 19:10) than that he should first befriend such sinners? As an aside, there is perhaps a lesson to be learnt here for those Christians who are so wrapped up in their Christian friendships that they have no unsaved friends left to whom they can witness.

Peter, as so often in the Gospels, can speak out about his friends: 'For you know that it was not with perishable things such as silver or gold that you were redeemed from the empty way of life handed down to you from your forefathers, but with the precious blood of Christ, a lamb *without blemish or defect* (1 Peter 1:18–19, emphasis mine).

Luke particularly testifies to Christ's perfection in his relationship with his parents. The incident of Jesus' absconding from the party returning from Jerusalem may have begun with confusion and a rebuke from his parents, but his explanation was so satisfactory that it became one of the things Mary 'treasured ... in her heart' (Luke 2:48–51). The preface to that comment is an unambiguous declaration that Jesus was observing the fifth commandment impeccably: 'Then he went down to Nazareth with them and was obedient to them' (Luke 2:51).

The next glimpse might not at first sight appear to sustain the point I am making but does so if we look a little deeper. In Luke 8 the evangelist records an instance when it was reported to Jesus that his family, including Mary, were nearby and seeking to speak with him. His response seems dismissive: 'He replied, "My mother and brothers are those who hear God's word and put it into practice"' (Luke 8:21). In reality, Jesus was merely stressing the priority of the spiritual over the natural in relationships. Our duty to our parents is not one to be evaded as the Pharisees were prone to do (Mark 7:9–13) but neither must it be allowed to compromise our proper service and devotion to God (Matthew 10:34–36). The grace of God is seen in the fact that at least three members of the

Saviour's earthly family were included in his spiritual one. Mary and 'his brothers' (note the plural) were counted among the disciples who constantly met together for prayer (Acts 1:14) and were presumably present and filled with the Holy Spirit on the Day of Pentecost. Paul tells us that 'James the Lord's brother' was among the apostles with whom he consulted after his conversion (Galatians 1:19). Jude, the author of the epistle, is designated the brother of James, most likely the one to whom we have just been referring, as no other James of any prominence was still alive at this time.

We turn to John's Gospel for our final evidence of exemplary filial duty. Jesus demonstrated a remarkable selflessness in that immediately prior to his death he spent time and care preparing the disciples for the ordeal that this event would be for them (John 13–18). Then in chapter 19 we read this poignant story: 'When Jesus saw his mother there, and the disciple whom he loved standing near by, he said to his mother, "Dear woman, here is your son," and to the disciple, "Here is your mother." From that time on, this disciple took her into his home' (John 19:26–27).

In the midst of his agony on the cross he made certain that Mary was entrusted into the care of one of his most trusted disciples, the only one brave and loyal enough to be there during his hours of suffering. A perfect son indeed!

Questions

COMPARING SCRIPTURE WITH SCRIPTURE

1. What light does the New Testament shed on the fifth commandment? (See Romans 1:29–32; Ephesians 6:1–4; Colossians 3:20; 1 Timothy 5:3–4; 2 Timothy 3:2.)

2. Read Exodus 1:22–2:8; 1 Samuel 1:27; Ruth 1:16–18; 2 Timothy 1:5 and 3:15. What can we learn from the example of these godly parents?

3. Is a godly child the inevitable result of a godly parent? See 1 Samuel 2:22–25 and 2 Samuel 16:20–22. What can be done to encourage such a result? See 1 Kings 3:14, 22:43 and 2 Chronicles 20:32.

APPLYING SCRIPTURE TO DAILY LIFE

1. How can we ensure that we strike the right balance between obeying our parents and obeying God?

2. In our modern world, where few family members live in close proximity to one another, how can adult children obey the fifth commandment in a practical way?

3. What place, if any, do vows have in the life of the Christian?

A different kind of judge

Foretold by God

Samson is different from the other judges of Israel in a number of ways. We have already noted the remarkable announcement of his birth by 'the angel of the LORD' that set him apart from the very outset.

'The angel of the LORD' had appeared at Bokim during the last days of Joshua, setting the scene for the tragic days that were to follow and which became known as the era of the judges (Judges 2:1,4). It is unclear from the reference to him in Deborah's song (Judges 5:23) how she was aware of the angel's presence at the battle recorded in chapter 4; Keil and Delitzsch comment that she 'heard from him the words of the curse upon the inhabitants of Meroz, because they did not come to help Jehovah when he was fighting with and for the Israelites'.[1] The text does not, however, tell us how that voice was made known. Block believes that it was in the form of a prophetic utterance from Deborah herself rather than the angel's physical presence, and he is probably correct.[2]

The next appearance of the angel of the LORD is in chapter 6, where he is instrumental in the calling of the reluctant Gideon to his role as judge and deliverer of his people. This incident, however, differs from that in chapter 13, where the judge Samson is not yet conceived: it is Samson's parents, not Samson himself, who are blessed by such a remarkable encounter.

The only other judge to consider is found outside of the book of Judges and forms the link between the judges and the kings of Israel—Samuel. Samuel's mother Hannah, like Samson's, was barren. Samuel's birth, however, was not so much foretold as prayed for by the old priest Eli (1 Samuel 1:17). Samson, then, is unique as far as the announcement of his birth and purpose under God are concerned.

Samson the loner

The second major difference is his solitary manner of action. The norm was that the judges, when raised up by God, summoned Israel to battle. This is what we see happening with Ehud (Judges 3:27–30), Deborah

(Judges 4), Gideon (Judges 7) and Jephthah (Judges 12:2), and it is strongly implied in the account of Othniel (Judges 3:10); the only other apparent exception is Shamgar whose entire history is recorded in one verse: 'After Ehud came Shamgar son of Anath, who struck down six hundred Philistines with an ox-goad. He too saved Israel' (Judges 3:31).

It must be granted that such a feat ranks alongside Samson's slaughter of 1,000 Philistines with the jawbone of an ass (Judges 15:15). We know too little about Shamgar and the other minor judges to make any valid comparisons. The narrative concerning Samson centres on his relationship with his enemies rather than his own people. The appearance of the men of Judah in chapter 15 seems to be almost incidental. Why Israel did not rally to this hero in their midst we do not know. His conflicts with the Philistines were always prompted by personal grievance rather than national exigency. This was not an accident; rather, it exposes for us the underlying problem and sheds light on the key comment in Judges 14:4: 'The LORD ... was seeking an occasion to confront the Philistines; for at that time they were ruling over Israel.' The people of God had grown complacent; they had made a servile peace with the Philistines. Their anxiety was not for deliverance, but that no one should 'rock the boat'. That God abhors this kind of complacent peace is made clear in the letter to Thyatira in the book of Revelation: 'Nevertheless, I have this against you: You *tolerate* that woman Jezebel, who calls herself a prophetess. By her teaching she misleads my servants into sexual immorality and the eating of food sacrificed to idols' (Revelation 2:20, emphasis mine).

Tolerance is regarded by many as the cardinal virtue in our present society. The United Nations' 'Declaration of Principles on Tolerance' contains the following phrase: 'Tolerance, the virtue that makes peace possible'.[3] God, however, is not primarily concerned about peace but about righteousness. Jesus said, 'Do not suppose that I have come to bring peace to the earth. I did not come to bring peace, but a sword' (Matthew 10:34). Paul took the church in Corinth to task for compromising the gospel by failing to discipline a member guilty of gross sexual immorality (1 Corinthians 5:9–12).

Some costs are too high to pay for mere peace. The sin and idolatry that accompanied Philistine rule was such a cost. We must always seek to reconcile the command to be peacemakers (Matthew 5:9) with the responsibilities of truth and holiness.

The person of Christ—foretold by God

There is a distinction between 'difference' and 'uniqueness': Samson was different; the Lord Jesus Christ was unique. I have never attempted, though I am sure someone has done so, to count the number of Old Testament passages that predict various aspects of the life and ministry of the Lord Jesus. Willmington's *Book of Bible Lists* records forty-five prophecies fulfilled by Christ during his earthly ministry, and that would only be the tip of the iceberg.4 His list includes Christ's birth and name (Isaiah 7:14), together with numerous descriptions of his ministry (e.g. Isaiah 6:9–10) and especially of his death (e.g. Psalm 34:20). The predictions concerning Christ commence in the very first book of the Bible:

So the LORD God said to the serpent, 'Because you have done this,
  Cursed are you above all the livestock
  and all the wild animals!
  You will crawl on your belly
  and you will eat dust
  all the days of your life.
  And I will put enmity
  between you and the woman,
  and between your offspring and hers;
  he will crush your head,
  and you will strike his heel' (Genesis 3:14–15).

Predictions concerning Christ are still to be found in the last chapter of the Bible, in relation to his future return: 'Behold, I am coming soon! My reward is with me, and I will give to everyone according to what he has done. I am the Alpha and the Omega, the First and the Last, the Beginning and the End' (Revelation 22:12–13).

His miraculous conception was announced to his mother by the angel Gabriel (Luke 1:26–38). The unborn John the Baptist leapt for joy in Elizabeth's womb at the sound of Mary's greeting (Luke 1:39–45). At the time of his birth an innumerable host of angels sang in unrestrained joy, to the amazement of some obscure Judean shepherds, while far to the east a star appeared that would guide the Magi across the miles until it rested over the place where the child now lay (Matthew 2). This is truly an announcement on a grand scale. Thirty years of obscurity passed before his public ministry was also heralded in a unique manner. His cousin John received divine revelation and proclaimed Jesus to be the long-awaited 'Lamb of God' (John 1:32–36). All of this is unprecedented, but a greater accolade was still to come: God the Father himself spoke audibly from heaven affirming his pleasure in Jesus, and God the Holy Spirit descended upon him visibly in the form of a dove (Matthew 3:16).

Jesus was indeed to judge, rule and deliver his people. There was a divine order in which these events had to occur. Firstly, he had to deliver them from their enemies. Paul expresses the change of rulers in this way: '... just as sin reigned in death, so also grace might reign through righteousness to bring eternal life through Jesus Christ our Lord' (Romans 5:21). Man prior to the death of Christ is ruled by a cruel coalition; Satan has blinded his eyes (2 Corinthians 4:4), he is mastered by sin (Romans 6:11–14) and lives his life in the fear of death (Hebrews 2:15). What Christ ushered in has radically changed the whole of creation:

The creation waits in eager expectation for the sons of God to be revealed. For the creation was subjected to frustration, not by its own choice, but by the will of the one who subjected it, in hope that the creation itself will be liberated from its bondage to decay and brought into the glorious freedom of the children of God (Romans 8:19–21).

Christ is truly the great deliverer offering salvation to those who repent and believe in him (Acts 2:36–40).

His judging, in the sense of ruling his people, has already begun, in that he is now 'far above all rule and authority, power and dominion, and every title that can be given, not only in the present age but also in the one to come' (Ephesians 1:21). It will find its ultimate fulfilment in the future when:

... at the name of Jesus every knee should bow,
  in heaven and on earth and under the earth,
and every tongue confess that Jesus Christ is Lord,
  to the glory of God the Father (Philippians 2:10–11).

Jesus—a loner?

We have seen that Samson was a loner. Jesus, by contrast, gathered around him a wide circle of followers and friends. We tend to think of his followers in terms of the twelve disciples, but on one occasion after his resurrection he appeared to more than 500 at one time (1 Corinthians 15:6). Within the twelve there was the privileged inner circle of Peter, James and John, who shared such momentous experiences as the transfiguration (Matthew 17:1–7). His plans were, however, on a much grander scale even than this. These were to be only the first of an innumerable company that, through the preaching of the gospel, was to come into a personal relationship with God through Christ. John was privileged to see the extent of the fulfilment of this plan, as part of the revelation granted to him by Christ:

After this I looked and there before me was a great multitude that no one could count, from every nation, tribe, people and language, standing before the throne and in front of the Lamb. They were wearing white robes and were holding palm branches in their hands. And they cried out in a loud voice:

'Salvation belongs to our God,
who sits on the throne,
and to the Lamb' (Revelation 7:9–10).

Christ died to redeem a *people* for himself, and to fashion them into his glorious church.

Questions

COMPARING SCRIPTURE WITH SCRIPTURE

1. What is the difference between the two great future judgements we see described in Revelation 20:11–15 and 2 Corinthians 5:10?

2. Consider the implications of being ruled by Christ as Paul sets them out in Colossians 1:9–14.

3. Using Genesis 3, consider the effect that sin has on relationships.

APPLYING SCRIPTURE TO DAILY LIFE

1. Our society is increasingly advocating tolerance (of different sexual orientations, religious beliefs, etc.) in such a way that a dissenting individual is no longer free to say 'this is wrong'. Such a position is itself inevitably 'intolerant'. What should be the Christian attitude to 'tolerance'?

2. How can we love sinners without tolerating their sin? How can we show this in our dealings with non-Christians?

3. Samson was a 'loner'. Is such a spiritual lifestyle desirable or even acceptable for a Christian? How significant is the church in the purposes of God?

Notes

1 C. F. Keil and F. Delitzsch, *Commentary on the Old Testament*, Vol. 2 (Peabody, MA: Hendrickson, 2002), p. 234.

2 D. I. Block, *Judges, Ruth*, The New American Commentary, Vol. 6 (Nashville: Broadman & Holman, 2001), p. 238.

3 http://unesdoc.unesco.org/images/0010/001018/101803e.pdf, p. 71 [accessed 24 February 2007].

4 H. L. Willmington, *Willmington's Book of Bible Lists* (Wheaton, IL: Tyndale House, 1987).

Chapter 6

The Timnite bride

Samson's women

There are three women in the life of Samson—all three are Philistines and all three are the cause of strife. As we have seen, their Philistine nationality (and, of course, religion) makes them unsuitable companions for a judge of Israel. Despite Gordon Keddie's objection[1] I would contend that the following prohibition is relevant:

When the LORD your God brings you into the land you are entering to possess and drives out before you many nations—the Hittites, Girgashites, Amorites, Canaanites, Perizzites, Hivites and Jebusites, seven nations larger and stronger than you—and when the LORD your God has delivered them over to you and you have defeated them, then you must destroy them totally. *Make no treaty with them*, and show them no mercy. *Do not intermarry with them.* Do not give your daughters to their sons or take their daughters for your sons, for they will turn your sons away from following me to serve other gods, and the LORD's anger will burn against you and will quickly destroy you. This is what you are to do to them: Break down their altars, smash their sacred stones, cut down their Asherah poles and burn their idols in the fire (Deuteronomy 7:1–5, emphasis mine).

This principle should be applied to marriage, which is a specific form of treaty. There is no reason to exclude the Philistines from the prohibition against intermarriage simply because they arrived in Canaan in significant numbers *after* the Israelite conquest. It surely applies as much to them as it did to those who preceded them.

A. C. Myers explains their presence and influence in Palestine in this way:

First rebuffed by the Egyptian pharaoh Merneptah ca. 1224–1211, apparently the Philistines began to settle on the Palestinian coastal plain after being defeated by Ramses III in a combined land and sea battle near the beginning of the twelfth century. Their territory eventually extended from Joppa to the Wâdī Ghazzeh. The coastal cities of Ashdod, Ashkelon, and Gaza, and the inland cities of Ekron and Gath, were the major Philistine population centres. The Philistines served as Egyptian mercenaries in the Nile delta, Nubia, and southwest Canaan, and apparently represented Egyptian power in Palestine until they became independent with the waning of Egyptian power in Asia in the eleventh and later centuries.

The Philistines were primarily warriors and did not displace the Canaanites whose territory they settled in. Instead, they adopted the culture of the Canaanites and became their rulers.[2]

Appendix A gives a much fuller account of these people.

His Timnite wife

There seems to be intended significance in the simple statements of Samson: 'I have seen' and 'get her for me'. The ESV[3] translation of 14:7 reads: 'Then he went down and talked with the woman, and she was *right in Samson's eyes*' (emphasis mine). Being a more literal translation than the NIV it better highlights what seems to be a deliberate play on words linking Samson's judgement with his physical sight. The attraction seems to be founded simply upon her pleasing appearance.

His wife's home is in Timnah,[4] located about five and a half miles west along the Sorek Valley from Samson's home in Zorah. Any confusion concerning the location of Timnah is easily explained once we note Block's explanation that 'Although it lay six miles straight west of Zorah, the description of Samson going down to Timnah is geographically accurate inasmuch as Timnah was located downstream from Zorah and Beth-Shemesh on the south side of the Wadi Sorek.'[5]

At this point we must address a more significant problem, namely that raised by the writer's comment in 14:4: 'His parents did not know that this was from the LORD, who was seeking an occasion to confront the Philistines; for at that time they were ruling over Israel.'

There are two possible interpretations: firstly, that Samson was aware of the underlying purposes of God and therefore acting in simple obedience. If this was so, then God was exercising his sovereign prerogative to set aside his own law for his own purpose; or, secondly, that

Samson was unaware and was acting disobediently. In this case God would have been acting despite the sinful intent of his servant, to nevertheless accomplish his own plan of inciting enmity between Samson/Israel and the Philistines.

The reader must choose. Both views have highly regarded supporters; for example, Matthew Henry[6] argues for the first understanding while John MacArthur[7] and Warren Wiersbe[8] argue for the second. My personal conviction lies with the second alternative. It better suits the text and offers fewer exegetical problems. Consequently, I believe this to be an example of God's gracious overruling despite disobedience.

So much is wrong with this marriage it is difficult to know where to start. We have already noted that the marriage was pursued against the express wishes of his parents. We also noted that the bride was a member of the despised race of 'uncircumcised Philistines', directly causing Samson to be 'yoked together with an unbeliever'—something Paul later expressly forbad (2 Corinthians 6:14).

The wedding feast itself seems innocent enough until one realizes that the word for feast, *mišteh,* in this context refers to a seven-day drinking bout at the home of the bride's parents. This picture of drunken revelry is an entirely realistic one. Block points out that among the most common types of pottery found by archaeologists in the Philistine settlements of Palestine are what he terms 'strainer-spout beer jugs'.[9] One may well question what a Nazirite and judge of Israel was doing in such company at all.

The woman herself proves unworthy, bowing to the threats and pressure of the 'companions' (14:15). She employs every emotional trick she knows to extract the answer to his riddle from him. Her motive is self-preservation; she chooses the safety of her father and herself above the interests of her husband. She exposes him to humiliation and ruin (thirty sets of clothing would cost a small fortune) in order to save herself. Her attempt tragically proves futile: her actions set off a 'tit for tat' exchange in which the level of violence escalates until, infuriated by their losses at the hands of Samson, the Philistines burn both her and her father to death (15:6). This action, far from ending the dispute, fires it still further and eventually unleashes two terrible bouts of slaughter at the hands of Samson

(15:7–8 and 15:15). The fear of violent death that caused her betrayal becomes a reality; tragically she gains nothing by her cowardice.

Samson the husband

There is clearly a lack of both tact and biblical understanding in Samson's comment to her, recorded in 14:16. His explanation as to why he had not let her in on the secret of the riddle is the unfeeling 'I haven't even explained it to my father or mother … so why should I explain it to you?' His attitude here is a far cry from the Genesis mandate: 'For this reason a man will leave his father and mother and be united to his wife, and they will become one flesh' (Genesis 2:24); it is also a salutary warning to all husbands and parents-in-law. If Samson is married to her, she, and not his parents, should now have the first claim on his confidence and trust.

The person of Christ

The picture of God as a husband is a common one in the Old Testament. It is expressly stated in Isaiah:

For your Maker is your husband—
   the LORD Almighty is his name—
the Holy One of Israel is your Redeemer;
   he is called the God of all the earth (54:5).

It is also stated in passages such as Jeremiah 3:14, 3:20, 31:32 and Hosea 2:16. The sin of Israel, particularly that of idolatry, is often described as adultery, an expression designed to evoke the imagery of marriage (Jeremiah 3:6–9; Ezekiel 23:37; Hosea 1:2). In particular, the book of Hosea contains a poignant account of the prophet's tragic marriage as a means of exposing the pain in the heart of God over Israel's apostasy.

As we move into the New Testament we find Christ portrayed as the perfect husband, with the church as the bride he is preparing for himself. Neither Samson's bride nor that of Christ (the church) seems either adequate or suitable. There is, however, a vital distinction to be made. The man Samson has no power to change his own sinful nature let alone that of his Timnite bride. The perfect God-man Christ Jesus, by contrast, can and will transform the church, making her fit for such an honour. The Apostle John was privileged to see this work accomplished as part of the revelation given to him on the island of Patmos. In Revelation 19 we see the bride perfected at last, and in the symbolic language typical of the book we read:

Then I heard what sounded like a great multitude, like the roar of rushing waters and like loud peals of thunder, shouting:

'Hallelujah!
For our Lord God Almighty reigns.
Let us rejoice and be glad
and give him glory!
For the wedding of the Lamb has come,
and his bride has made herself ready.
Fine linen, bright and clean,
was given her to wear'
(fine linen stands for the righteous acts of the saints) (Revelation 19:6–8).

Paul ends his extended teaching on the relationship between husbands and wives (Ephesians 5:22–33) with the observation: 'This is a profound mystery—but I am talking about Christ and the church.' In doing so he sets all of his wisdom on family life in the context of the perfect example of Jesus. It is his sacrificial love that all husbands must emulate. Wives, who must willingly submit to their husbands, would surely find their responsibility so much easier if their men were more Christlike.

Questions

COMPARING SCRIPTURE WITH SCRIPTURE

1. What do we learn from the following passages about the 'husband' love of God? See Jeremiah 3:14; 3:20; 31:32; and Hosea 2:16.

2. Why does God view sin, especially that of idolatry, as spiritual adultery? See Jeremiah 3:6–9; Ezekiel 23:37; and Hosea 1:2.

3. What are the characteristics of the 'bride' in Revelation 19:1–9?

APPLYING SCRIPTURE TO DAILY LIFE

1. How can husbands better reflect the perfect husband, Christ? How should this affect the way they treat their wives?

2. What is 'submission' as referred to by Paul in Ephesians 5?

3. Should wives be 'subject' to their imperfect human husbands? What does this mean in practice?

Notes

1 **Keddie,** *Even in Darkness,* pp. 93–94.

2 **Myers,** *The Eerdmans Bible Dictionary,* p. 829.

3 *The Holy Bible: English Standard Version* (Wheaton, IL: Standard Bible Society, 2001).

4 **V. H. Matthews, M. W. Chavalas and J. H. Walton,** *The IVP Bible Background Commentary: Old Testament* (electronic ed.), Judges 14:1 (Downers Grove, IL: InterVarsity Press, 2000).

5 **Block,** *Judges, Ruth,* p. 424.

6 **M. Henry,** *Matthew Henry's Commentary on the Whole Bible: Complete and unabridged in one volume,* Judges 14:4 (Peabody: Hendrickson, 1996).

7 **J. J. MacArthur,** *The MacArthur Study Bible* (electronic ed.), Judges 14:1 (Nashville: Word, 1997).

8 **Wiersbe,** *Be Available,* p. 110.

9 See **T. and M. Dothan,** *People of the Sea: The Search for the Philistines* (New York: Macmillan, 1992), pp. 90, 134. Quoted by **Block,** *Judges, Ruth,* p. 431.

The man of strength

He-man?

The popular picture of Samson, reinforced by illustrated children's books, is of a muscular he-man who has spent much of his time 'working out'—a kind of Arnold Schwarzenegger figure. One commentator even refers to him as 'the biblical counterpart of Hercules'.[1]

If there is any link at all with Hercules, it is that the Hercules narratives are a clear mythologizing of biblical history. The Bible, however, gives us no physical description of Samson other than the length of his hair. It is unlikely, but not impossible, that he was a 7-stone (98 lb) weakling. His strength came not from physical prowess but a direct endowment from God. He was strong when 'the Spirit of the LORD' was upon him; then, and only then, was he invincible.

Mighty exploits

The catalogue of his mighty deeds is certainly impressive and they permeate his entire story. Chapter 14 shows us the first two of these exploits and their significance.

SLAYING THE LION (14:5–6)

This is the first of these recorded mighty deeds. Despite being an amazing feat of strength, Samson not merely killing the lion but tearing it in pieces, the incident is described in just two verses. It seems to be recorded more for its later significance in the matter of the wedding riddle (14:14) than for its own intrinsic value. Samson, not noted for his modesty (see 15:16), nevertheless, as we noted above, does not bother to mention it to his parents. Two things need to be observed here: firstly, this miracle, for miracle it undoubtedly is, is directly attributed to the power of the Spirit of the Lord who is said to have 'rushed upon' Samson; secondly, we see the providential hand of God, a subject that will occupy our thoughts later. Samson's silence serves the purposes of God that are yet to be revealed. Samson seems to act with casual disdain; the incident is recorded as if it were of little importance. So mighty is the hand of God when it rests upon his servant that even spectacular events assume an air of the ordinary. There is evidence of this phenomenon elsewhere in Scripture. Consider for a moment the simple statement in Acts 19:11 that 'God did extraordinary miracles through Paul', then take a moment to absorb what you have just read. What an incredible use of words! If these miracles were 'extraordinary', the implication is that there was in those days such a thing as an 'ordinary miracle'!

At this point we are getting a little ahead of ourselves and need to go back to the narrative to consider some things that we have so far passed over. As we study the story of Samson we are soon forced to abandon any picture of him as a muscle-bound numbskull. Rather, he emerges as a man of considerable innate intelligence who is nevertheless capable of spectacular stupidity when governed by his passions rather than his head.

SAMSON'S RIDDLE (14:14)

When Samson arrives at Timnah for his wedding he is confronted by the intimidating presence of thirty Philistine 'companions'. The purpose of God, made explicit in 14:4—to break Israel's unholy acquiescence in Philistine domination—is about to take a giant leap forward. Samson seeks to humiliate and impoverish his 'companions' in one fell swoop. His method is a cleverly constructed riddle. Only he is aware of the events of 14:6–9; even his parents are unaware that the honey he offered them was taken from the carcass of a lion he had slain. The riddle Samson poses is extremely clever in more ways than one. In early Hebrew the same word can mean both 'lion' and 'honey'.[2] Furthermore the riddle ('Out of the eater, something to eat; out of the strong, something sweet') is unanswerable without the key, which, as we have seen, Samson alone possesses. He has the Philistines in the palm of his hand. This clever plan is, however, brought to nothing, the tables are turned, and humiliation is heaped upon him rather than upon the Philistines. Samson is naive enough to give his new bride the ammunition to betray him; her tears blind him to the truth of her insincerity and he is betrayed. His response is twofold; he signals his awareness of the situation with a poetic turn of phrase, responding to their rhyme with another one of his own:

Before sunset on the seventh day the men of the town said to him,
'What is sweeter than honey?
What is stronger than a lion?'
Samson said to them,
'If you had not ploughed with my heifer,
you would not have solved my riddle' (14:18).

There is a deep irony to Samson's riddle, for at the end of his life the Philistines set him to grind corn for them to eat and from that punishment he tasted the sweetness of revenge.

THE MASSACRE AT ASHKELON (14:19)

This second feat shares two significant features with the first exploit: the extreme brevity of the account (just one verse on this occasion), and the repetition of the vital information that this was again achieved because 'the Spirit of the LORD came upon him in power'. The reader may at this point find questions of morality rising in his or her mind. Why would the Spirit of the Lord enable Samson to kill thirty seemingly innocent men in order to pay off a gambling debt?

We will understand something of what is happening when we consider the statement in 14:4: 'that this was from the LORD, who was seeking an occasion to confront the Philistines; for at that time they were ruling over Israel'. This verse is pivotal to our understanding of so much in the Samson story that we will find ourselves referring to it again and again. The Philistines were not, of course, in the eyes of a holy God, 'innocent men'. As individuals they were, like all men, sinners by nature and therefore justly under the wrath and condemnation of Almighty God. Their individual culpability is not disclosed in any detail; however, we may be sure that on this occasion, as on every occasion, Abraham's confidence would have been vindicated: 'Far be it from you to do such a thing—to kill the righteous with the wicked, treating the righteous and the wicked alike. Far be it from you! Will not the Judge of all the earth do right?' (Genesis 18:25).

Further we must remember that they were part of an oppression of the people of God that Samson had been raised up to bring to an end. This was the start of that campaign.

The person of Christ

Samson was dependent on the power of the Holy Spirit to achieve his mighty exploits. When the Spirit departed from him he was as weak as any mortal man. The situation with Jesus was, of course, different in a number of significant ways. As the second person of the Trinity Jesus possessed all the power of the Godhead by divine right. What we see during his earthly ministry is a voluntary setting aside of those powers and a self-imposed reliance upon the Holy Spirit for the performance of all his miracles. We can assert this on the authority of history: he performed no mighty deeds until he was endued with the Spirit's power at his baptism (Matthew 3:1–11; Mark 1:3–8; Luke 3:2–17). It was only after this event that his ministry commenced (Luke 3:23). We also have the explicit teaching of the apostles, notably in Philippians 2:1–11. Here Paul uses such phrases as 'but made himself nothing', which clearly teach that this limitation was of his own volition. This self-limitation forms a vital part of his relationship to us in so many different ways.

The Holy Spirit was given to the church as a coronation gift of the risen Christ (Ephesians 3:14–20) so that we can live our lives in dependence on him as our Saviour did. Jesus is our great and sympathetic High Priest (Hebrews 4:14–15) and our confidence in him is enhanced by the knowledge that he, like us, relied on the Word of God and the Spirit's power to overcome temptation (Matthew 4:1–11; Mark 1:12–13; Luke 4:1–13). The story of Samson tantalizes us with the prospect of what a man empowered by God could achieve; the life of Christ shows us the reality in glorious technicolour.

Questions

COMPARING SCRIPTURE WITH SCRIPTURE

1. What is Paul telling us in Ephesians 6:12?
2. Consider the implications of Christ's words in John 15:5.
3. What can we learn from the confidence of the psalmist in such passages as Psalm 60:12 and 108:13?

APPLYING SCRIPTURE TO DAILY LIFE

1. How should Ephesians 6:12 affect our attitude to those who oppose the gospel? Should it affect the way we respond to them, and if so, how?

2. Sin severely limited the usefulness of Samson. Is this always its effect? What practical lessons can we learn from this?

3. How can we live our lives in greater dependence on the Holy Spirit?

Notes

1 L. Ryken, J. Wilhoit, T. Longman, C. Duriez, D. Penney and D. G. Reid, *Dictionary of Biblical Imagery* (electronic ed.) (Downers Grove, IL: InterVarsity Press, 2000), p. 754.

2 H. Baur, quoted by Kim, *The Structure of the Samson Cycle*, p. 252.

A never-ending cycle

Samson seems to be unaware of the basic laws of cause and effect. Sometime after the events of chapter 14 he returns to Timnah armed with the peace offering of a young goat—the rough equivalent, no doubt, of a box of chocolates or a nice bunch of flowers. He clearly expects to patch things up with his wife and resume his relationship with her. He is not merely surprised but is outraged to discover that his father-in-law has made the entirely reasonable assumption that his departure was permanent. Acting on that assumption he has given his daughter to one of the so-called 'friends' who were at the wedding. Our modern sensibilities are probably offended at the chauvinistic way in which Samson is offered her younger and allegedly more attractive sister as compensation; there is, however, ample evidence that such treatment was far from rare, the deception of Laban in the story of Jacob, Rachel and Leah being a prime example (Genesis 29).

This time Samson's revenge is both focused and planned; he takes the time to capture the animals he needs and deploys them to maximum effect.

The four-footed arsonists (15:1–5)

Many scholars argue that the creatures referred to here were probably jackals rather than foxes, the latter being solitary animals and consequently unlikely to have been present in sufficient numbers.[1] Samson inflicts a severe economic penalty on his enemies. He chooses the optimum time and highly advantageous locations. The effect is that the harvested corn is destroyed alongside that which is still growing, and as a bonus, the vineyards and olive trees are also ruined. He is clearly capable of strategy as well as blind rage.

This and the sequel in 15:8 are among the few 'mighty deeds' performed by Samson that are not directly said to have been accomplished by the power of the Spirit. Nevertheless, we may safely assume that both of them were accomplished by divine power. The difficulties in capturing and controlling such animals would prove excessive, if not impossible, without God's intervention. Furthermore, the event advances the previously stated intent of God, 'who was seeking an occasion to confront the Philistines' (14:4). The probability is that Samson was always possessed of great strength, which God miraculously supplemented when even greater prowess was needed. The havoc caused would have rendered a severe blow to the Philistine economy and, if you will excuse the pun, lit a flame of hope in Israel.

Revenge, and yet more revenge (15:6–8)

Once again the consequences of his actions seem to be unexpected to Samson, who sees his canine attack merely as 'getting even' (15:3) rather than unleashing the escalating conflict that God intended. The reaction of the Philistines is typical of fallen man: having identified the 'Timnite's son-in-law' as the culprit (15:6), they conveniently forget that Samson's wife was coerced and threatened into betraying him in the matter of the riddle. There is a deep tragedy unfolding here; each party acts wrongly in hope of gain and each loses the very thing for which they strive. The Philistines are afraid of losing face and wealth, and lose both; Samson's bride, fearing for her life, sets in motion a train of events that results in the death of both her and her family. Ironically, that death is by fire, the very fate she betrayed Samson in order to evade. Not only do the ends not justify wrong means; wrong means also sometimes, as here, spectacularly fail to achieve the ends.

The person of Christ

The ministry of Christ is nowhere more challenging than on this issue of revenge. Homer could not have summed up the popular viewpoint more aptly when he said that revenge 'is sweeter far than flowing honey'.[2] One feels that both Samson and the Philistines would have voiced a hearty 'amen' to such a sentiment. Sadly, both lived long enough to prove the more accurate observation of John Milton: 'Revenge, at first though sweet, Bitter ere long back on itself recoils.'[3] The Bible is full of the frantic search for revenge by those who have been, or perceive themselves to be, victims of some injustice. Haman is a prime example,[4] but others abound. It is a desire God set strict limitations on in Israel by the creation of 'cities of refuge' (see Numbers 35). These were created so that those guilty of what we would term 'manslaughter', rather than premeditated murder, would have somewhere to flee from the 'avenger of blood'; once there they would have the protection of God's Law.

Jesus, however, took the subject into a whole new, and more challenging, realm. That this teaching was vitally needed is evidenced by the note of glee in the disciples' misplaced offer: 'Lord, do you want us to call fire down from heaven to destroy them?' (Luke 9:51–55) This excess of zeal surprisingly emanated from no greater offence than a Samaritan village's snub in failing to offer hospitality to Jesus and his followers. Christ's teaching was peppered with disturbing commands and illustrations; the Lord's Prayer includes the petition, 'Forgive us our debts, as we also have forgiven our debtors', with the accompanying explanation: 'For if you forgive men when they sin against you, your heavenly Father will also forgive you. But if you do not forgive men their sins, your Father will not forgive your sins' (Matthew 6:9–15).

Peter's somewhat self-congratulatory boast of forgiving seven times was rebuffed with the Saviour's memorable story of the unforgiving servant (Matthew 18:21–35). His declaration that we must forgive seventy times seven was clearly not intended to indicate that after 490 (carefully counted) instances of mercy we can then give vent to our repressed anger; rather, Jesus was commanding infinite mercy. Pithy sayings such as 'Love your enemies' (Matthew 5:44) were crowned with his own supreme example. As he suffered an agonizing death on the cross, the Saviour only made seven utterances, one of those being: 'Father, forgive them, for they do not know what they are doing' (Luke 23:34). This new approach to an age-old problem became mainstream Christian teaching. Paul, for instance, when writing to the church in Rome, urged them:

Do not repay anyone evil for evil. Be careful to do what is right in the eyes of everybody. If it is possible, as far as it depends on you, live at peace with everyone. Do not take revenge, my friends, but leave room for God's wrath, for it is written: 'It is mine to avenge; I will repay,' says the Lord. On the contrary:

'If your enemy is hungry, feed him;
if he is thirsty, give him something to drink.

In doing this, you will heap burning coals on his head.'
Do not be overcome by evil, but overcome evil with good (Romans 12:17–21).

We must each carefully examine our own lives to discover how faithfully we follow the Lord in these significant and practical areas.

Questions

COMPARING SCRIPTURE WITH SCRIPTURE

1. What can we learn about the proper balance between justice and mercy from Numbers 35?

2. What do we learn about the consequences of seeking revenge from the story of Samson?

3. From Romans 12:17–21, what do we learn about right *attitudes* and *actions* towards others?

APPLYING SCRIPTURE TO DAILY LIFE

1. Can there be forgiveness without repentance?

2. What is the difference between showing mercy and granting forgiveness?

3. Is it possible to follow Christ with an unforgiving heart? Are there issues in your own life you need to deal with in this regard?

Notes

1 The Hebrew word *šû'ā lîm* was used of both foxes and jackals. Since the latter were more common in Palestine, and since foxes are solitary animals, Samson probably was dealing with jackals. Jackals are certainly intended in Ezekiel 13:4, Lamentations 5:18 and Psalm 63:10, where the same word is used. Quoted by Block, *Judges, Ruth*, p. 36.

2 *The Iliad* (XVIII, 109) http://www.worldofquotes.com/topic/Revenge/1/index.hmtl [accessed 16 September 2006].

3 **John Milton,** *Paradise Lost*, Book IX, l. 171.

4 See the author's book *Exploring Esther* (Leominster: Day One Publications, 2005).

Battles, and yet more battles

Making donkeys of the Philistines (15:8–20)

The final climactic battle at Lehi brings this cycle of vengeance to a temporary end. Following his vicious slaughter of the Philistines (15:8) Samson retreats to a cave in Etam; he is, however, pursued by the Philistines, who spread out in battle lines, threatening the inhabitants of the Hebrew settlement at Lehi. The unusual nature of this aggression perturbs the men of Judah; hitherto their subservience has guaranteed a measure of peace and stability. Samson is identified as the cause and the men of Judah take the coward's path. Sadly, rather than seeking the leadership of the mighty Samson to combat the threat, the 3,000 men of Judah determine to deliver their judge into the clutches of their enemies. This is foolish as well as cowardly. They are more concerned to save their own skins than to seize an opportunity to gain renown as others had done before them. This is their chance to follow God's anointed judge into battle and secure victory over their enemies. Victory is never the reward of the fainthearted.

The naivety of Samson is evidenced in his response to the reasonable question, 'Don't you realize that the Philistines are rulers over us? What have you done to us?' (15:11). His answer is inadequate: 'I merely did to them what they did to me.' This hardly fits the facts.

At the time of writing this chapter (August 2006) the newspapers are full of debate about the conflict between the state of Israel and the terrorist organization Hezbollah. What began with the kidnap of two Israeli soldiers has escalated into a bloody conflict that has engulfed Israel's neighbour, Lebanon. One area of debate concerns the response of Israel to that event and whether it can be justified as being 'proportional' to the provocation. Similarly, Samson's explanation seems unsatisfactory. Samson has indeed suffered; he has been betrayed, lied to, humiliated and has lost his wife, firstly to the arms of another man and then through her cruel murder. However, his response to this suffering has already cost the lives of the thirty men of Ashkelon and then he attacked the Philistines '*viciously* and slaughtered *many* of them' (emphasis mine). He might have justified his attacks on the grounds of God's purposes, or as a response to the injustices heaped on his people by their oppressors, but not on account of his personal injury, however real. Cicero's maxim, 'Justice is the crowning glory of the virtues', seems clearly to have been breached.[1]

The incident has particular significance as it is the only occasion on which we see the solitary Samson interacting with his fellow Israelites. There is also both wisdom and compassion in this section of the narrative. We discover a fresh aspect of Samson's character—his concern for his own people. It is hardly credible that his extracting of the promise (15:12) that the men of Judah will not kill him is motivated by simple fear for his own life. If that were so he would be infinitely better facing them than the Philistines. There are two possible explanations for his concern. It may be that he is unsure that the divine power he would need to overcome such odds would be granted if the recipients were God's own people rather than their enemies. More likely it is concern for their well-being that moves him at this moment. If they try to kill him he can certainly defend himself, but only at the cost of their blood. Either way he has a plan.

Eliciting from them a pledge that they will not seek to injure him themselves, he placidly submits to their bonds. The following narrative is both poetic and graphic: strong bonds snap like cotton and with the aid of an improvised cudgel Samson slaughters 1,000 of his enemies. The small detail that the jawbone was 'fresh' (15:15) is a mark of the authenticity and historicity of the story—an old bone would have been brittle and unsuitable as a weapon.

It is after this great victory that we are told of Samson's twenty-year judgeship, a period during which he seems to have been at liberty to move among the Philistines unhindered, such is the fear they have of him. Indeed, the next incident places him some forty-five miles away from home and deep in Philistine country.

The person of Christ

The moral highlight of this passage is the compassion of Samson for his own people. He is faced with a clear choice: hazarding his own life or forfeiting theirs. To his credit he embraces the sentiment of Romans 12:10

and chooses the welfare of others over his own. Such a sacrificial spirit is not without precedent in Scripture; Ruth typifies it in her selfless devotion to her mother-in-law Naomi (see the book of Ruth, especially 1:16–17). David has the same spirit when he defies the convention that after a coup you kill all the descendants of the previous king (See 1 Kings 15:28–29). Instead he preserves the life of Saul's grandson Mephibosheth and grants him lifelong security (2 Samuel 9:1–13).

Compassion was one of the motivating forces in the life and ministry of Christ, as explicitly stated in Matthew: 'Jesus went through all the towns and villages, teaching in their synagogues, preaching the good news of the kingdom and healing every disease and sickness. When he saw the crowds, he had compassion on them, because they were harassed and helpless, like sheep without a shepherd' (9:35–36). The following verses make it clear that the command to the disciples to pray for workers to be thrust out into the work of evangelism sprang from that same deep well. Compassion was the reason, Matthew tells us, why Jesus healed the sick (Matthew 14:14), fed the hungry (Matthew 15:32), and gave sight to the blind (Matthew 20:34). Paul listed it as a direct fruit of the believer's fellowship with Christ (Philippians 2:1), and a virtue with which we must seek to be clothed (Colossians 3:12). Little wonder that James, in his letter, reminds us that 'the Lord is full of compassion and mercy' (James 5:11).

The life of Jesus was one continuous example of putting the needs of others before his own. Illustrations of this are so numerous it is difficult to know which to choose. The incarnation itself was a voluntary abandonment of what Jesus referred to in prayer as 'the glory I had with you [the Father] before the world began' (John 17:5). We have already mentioned Gethsemane (Matthew 26:36–46), which revealed the extent of that prioritizing of others. There we behold Jesus, fully aware of both the physical and spiritual torment that awaits him, subjecting his will to the Father's on our behalf. Ultimately, of course, it was to be seen at the cross. Paul put it beautifully when he described Jesus as 'the Son of God, who loved me and gave himself for me' (Galatians 2:20).

Chapter 9

Questions

1. How is the compassion of God evident in Deuteronomy 34:1–7?

2. What characteristics of compassion are seen in the following passages: Psalm 86:15–17; 119:156; Isaiah 49:8–26?

3. How are we to understand Romans 9:14?

APPLYING SCRIPTURE TO DAILY LIFE

1. Samson's great purpose was to set the people of Israel free from Philistine oppression. What oppresses men and women today? (See Luke 4:18; Romans 6:16–23; Hebrews 2:15.)

2. How is compassion gained and shared according to 2 Corinthians 1:3–11?

3. In what practical ways can we implement Ephesians 4:32 and 1 Peter 3:8–9?

Note

1 Marcus Tullius Cicero (Ancient Roman lawyer, writer, scholar, orator and statesman, 106 BC–43 BC. See http://en.thinkexist.com/quotations/justice/2.html [accessed 24 August 2006].

Danger in Gaza

The prostitute in Gaza

This section introduces us to Gaza, the city destined to be the scene of Samson's eventual captivity, death and ultimate feat of strength and deliverance. Gaza was one of the five city states that together formed the Philistine coalition. Situated three miles from the Mediterranean Sea and on the highest vantage point in the area, it was the premier city during the Armarna period. Modern archaeology has as yet uncovered little of the 135-acre site depicted in various Egyptian reliefs.

Samson's choice of women does not improve: first an unnamed wife betrayed him and now an unnamed prostitute leads him into both moral and physical danger. Once again his eyes are his downfall, and his passions indulged without restraint. For Samson, 'to see' seems to be 'to desire', and 'to desire' means 'to get'. He never appears to consider the potential consequences. The story is marked by the casual nature of the event: he just happens to see her. There is no premeditation, rather a flippant disdain for the Law of God. If we are shocked, and we should be, that a judge of Israel would visit a prostitute at all, we must sadly note that such liaisons were far from uncommon in the history of the Old Testament. Judah visited one (Genesis 38:15–16); Jephthah's mother was one (Judges 11:1); they were obviously common during the rules of Solomon (1 Kings 3:16) and Ahab (1 Kings 22:38); Hosea suffered the personal tragedy of his wife degenerating into prostitution (Hosea 3:3); Ezekiel was familiar with their presence in the land of exile (Ezekiel 16:33; 23:44); and the writer of Proverbs saw the need for repeated warnings to the youth of his day on the dangers of consorting with them (Proverbs 6:26; 7:10; 23:27; and 29:3). The most disturbing of all, perhaps, was Joel's exposure to the oppression in his own day that led to a situation in which:

They cast lots for my people
　and traded boys for prostitutes;

they sold girls for wine
    that they might drink (Joel 3:3).

That prostitution was common does not mean it was condoned by God. It was explicitly condemned in the Law which levelled heavy penalties on those who practised it (Leviticus 19:29; 21:9; Deuteronomy 23:18). Most telling of all is the fact that the majority of references to prostitution are those that use it as an illustration of the sin of departing from the worship of God (Exodus 34:15–16; Leviticus 17:7; 20:6; Numbers 15:39; Deuteronomy 31:16; 1 Chronicles 5:25; 2 Chronicles 21:11–13; Jeremiah 2:20; 3:1–3; Ezekiel 16:15–35; 23:3–44). Occasionally the two intersect because of the prevalence of cultic prostitution. Male and female prostitutes were an essential part of the perverted 'fertility worship' of Canaanite idols. How unwise Samson's passions make him; how true the words of Proverbs prove to be in his life:

Do not lust in your heart after her beauty
    or let her captivate you with her eyes,
for the prostitute reduces you to a loaf of bread,
    and the adulteress preys upon your very life (Proverbs 6:25–26).

Somehow his presence is discovered and he is betrayed. It seems likely that the culprit was the prostitute herself, but this is not certain. The Philistines lay a plan to capture him. They will lie in wait until dawn and then spring their trap. The old Chinese proverb 'Not until just before dawn do people sleep best' has found an echo in the hearts of many a military strategist.[1] Dawn is the time when a man is most vulnerable, half asleep and half awake; it is the ideal moment for a surprise attack. The men of Gaza knew they would need every edge they could get if they were to prevail over this mighty enemy. Samson, however, thwarts their plan and, whether he is aware of the plot or not, makes good his escape.

The removal man
On this occasion he saves his life by carrying the gates of the city away with him. It is a truly spectacular feat to detach and carry away the gates

of a city like Gaza. Such gates were often of considerable height and as much as twelve feet in width.[2] Made of the densest wood available they consequently weighed a considerable amount. These gates were attached to posts set into stone sockets and sunk deep into the ground. They would be locked at night and remain barred until the morning. They were constructed to be substantial enough to protect the inhabitants from any would-be assailant. The Hebrew text at this point is problematic[3] and the narrative poses many questions by its sheer brevity; it is, however, another clear example of Samson's incredible prowess. Even if he did not carry the gates the whole forty miles back into the heart of Israelite territory but deposited them on some hillside along the way, to remove them at all is an amazing achievement. He defiantly plants them like a trophy on the top of a hill facing Hebron and, in so doing, again humiliates his adversaries.

The person of Christ

There are only two direct references in the Gospels to prostitutes. One is a detail in the story of the Prodigal Son and forms part of the bitter recrimination of the elder brother occasioned by his father's welcome for the wayward younger son (Luke 15:30). The young man's life in the far country clearly included frequent and expensive visits to prostitutes. It was a significant part of the lifestyle from which he was delivered only after extreme poverty and hardship had brought him to his senses. Such liaisons with prostitutes had formed a real part of what he had come to see as his sin against God and his father's love.

The other reference to prostitutes forms part of the application to another parable about two sons (Matthew 21:28–32). Here, there is something to celebrate as well as something to lament. The celebration is because prostitutes and tax collectors are entering the kingdom of God; the sadness is occasioned by the blind refusal of the chief priests and elders to repent, believe and find forgiveness, as those they so despised were doing.

Though references to prostitution are sparse, there are, however, notable instances of Jesus dealing with other immoral women. In John we read the account of the Samaritan woman, isolated from her own people as a result of her notorious lifestyle. Her conversation with the Saviour so transformed her life that many believed as a direct result of her testimony. John also records in 7:53–8:11⁴ the account of a woman caught in adultery; again it is a story which ends on a note of hope and restoration. The woman, instead of being stoned to death, is forgiven by the only one with authority to do so. Self-righteous religious people are given a salutary insight into their own hearts and the clear mandate is delivered: 'Go now and leave your life of sin.' While Samson was involved with the exploitation of these women (and however willing prostitutes may seem, in reality they are an abused, vulnerable and exploited group of people), Jesus was involved in their most profound welfare. They were among the lost he came to seek and to save (Luke 19:10).

Questions

COMPARING SCRIPTURE WITH SCRIPTURE

1. Read Proverbs 6:26 and 7:6–27. What are the consequences of following Samson's example and visiting a prostitute?

2. Read Proverbs 23:26–28, Job 31:1–4, 2 Samuel 11 and Matthew 5:27–30. What do these passages teach us about where the battle for purity must begin?

APPLYING SCRIPTURE TO DAILY LIFE

1. Read 1 Corinthians 6:15–17. What do you think are the implications of Paul's teaching here about sexual union? How does it apply to other forms of sexual contact such as pre-marital sex, same-sex unions and multiple sexual partners (all of which are common in our present society)?

2. Read 1 Corinthians 6:9–11. What does this passage teach us about the power of the gospel?

Notes

1   http://www.quotationspage.com/search.php3?Search=Dawn&startsearch=Search&Author=
    &C=mgm&C=motivate&C=classic&C=coles&C=poorc&C=lindsly[accessed 16 September
    2006].

2 Matthews, Chavalas, and Walton, *The IVP Bible Background Commentary.*

3 See the detailed treatment in **Block,** *Judges, Ruth*, p. 449.

4 See Chapter 11 note 3.

Samson and Delilah

Delilah

Delilah is unique among Samson's women for a number of reasons. She is the only one to be named. Neither his wife nor the prostitute from Gaza is given this degree of significance. Scripture often signifies its disdain of individuals by not naming them. None of the rulers of Egypt is specifically named, but is merely referred to by the title 'Pharaoh'.

Delilah is the only woman Samson is said to have loved. Better words can be found to describe his other attachments. The Timnite seems to infatuate him: he desires her but does not love her in any meaningful way. He lusts after the prostitute; she is an object, a thing to be used then discarded and forgotten. Delilah he loves, but she does not love him. As chapter 16 opened Samson was seen 'using' the prostitute for his own sexual gratification; now it is Delilah who is using him as a path to riches. Now it is he who will be discarded once his purpose has been fulfilled. How far mankind has fallen from the elation Adam felt on first seeing his Eve! She was what he longed for in the depths of his soul, a mate perfectly fitted to match him. She was what made him complete and whole. Sin has certainly exacted a fearful price in this most intimate of relationships.

Samson's liaison with Delilah seems to last longer than with any of the other women. There is ample time for three abortive attempts at his capture prior to the nagging that went on 'day after day' (v. 16), finally breaking his resistance and sealing his fate.

It is sad that in the popular mind it is this affair above all that defines Samson. When in 1949 Cecil B. DeMille wanted to make a Hollywood epic of the story, he chose to name it *Samson and Delilah*, and gave star billing to Hedy Lamar (Delilah) over Victor Mature (Samson), George Sanders and Angela Lansbury. The storyline to the 1996 remake read like this: 'Samson is a strong man, who is fighting against the Philistines. These have occupied the land of Canaan. Then Samson meets Delilah, a Philistine woman. She devised a plan, to destroy the Israelite.'[1] As usual with Hollywood, the scripts bear little resemblance to the Scripture original.

Samson here is not the God-ordained judge of Israel but the plaything of a scheming woman. Tragically, he brought much of this popular myth upon himself.

Delilah follows the pattern set by the Timnite wife; she too wears down the strong man with unceasing nagging in order to betray him to her own people. In one respect at least she is worse than the Timnite, who had to be threatened with death before she would agree to betray Samson; all Delilah requires is the promise of wealth. The significance that Samson had can be seen in two details recorded in 16:5. Firstly, all five rulers of the Philistines seem to make their offer in person to Delilah. Secondly, the financial inducement they offer is stunningly large. We can gain some idea of how much she was paid by looking at the incident related in 2 Samuel 18. There Joab rebukes a soldier for missing his opportunity to kill King David's rebel son, Absalom. Joab boasts that he would have given the man ten shekels of silver, but is told that such a deed would not have been committed even for a thousand shekels (vv. 11–12). Here, each of the Philistine lords is offering Delilah 1,100 shekels—a total of 5,500. To put it another way, she is offered 550 years' wages to betray Israel's judge! This offer alone tells us how much of a thorn in the flesh Samson had become.

Two verses from Proverbs seem particularly apt in summing up Samson, his women and their legacy: 'For the lips of an adulteress drip honey, and her speech is smoother than oil' (5:3); and 'A foolish son is his father's ruin, and a quarrelsome wife is like a constant dripping' (19:13). The man who cannot be subdued, not even by 1,000 armed Philistines baying for blood, is rendered pathetically helpless by his own fatal attraction to ungodly women.

Deliverance from Delilah's traps

His liaison with Delilah leads to three further feats of strength for us to consider. (We will look at the final, and greatest, exhibition of his might in the next chapter.) Having fallen in love with Delilah, Samson finds himself systematically deceived in her repeated attempts to discover the 'secret of his great strength' (16:5). He seeks to placate her with false answers: seven fresh thongs, new ropes and weaving the seven braids of his hair onto a loom. All are tested and found false as she cries out, 'The Philistines are upon you!' (16:9,12,14). Samson simply brushes aside the impediments as if they are nothing. The incidents are petty and serve to show how far Samson has fallen. No victory is gained against his enemies and no purpose of delivery is served. They form a fitting prelude to his capture and consequent imprisonment.

These sad scenes are also the backdrop to the most poignant verse in the entire story. Weakened by the constant pleading, Samson reveals his secret. He is sheared like some pathetic sheep and this time when the cry rings out again, 'The Philistines are upon you!' he rises as he always has done, unconcerned, and perhaps a little amused. But this is an occasion like no other he has ever known—the Lord is no longer with him. Everything in his life is different because the God of Israel, his shield and his strength, has departed. Samson is alone; he is a mere man stripped of the power of his God. What glee there must have been among his enemies as they rained down blow after blow and received no significant reply! The narrator simply records, 'But he did not know that the LORD had left him' (16:20). In those few words we are reminded of the source of Samson's strength, the depth of his fall and the penalty to be paid for sin. We might wish to reflect with equal sadness that the same can be true of individuals, churches and entire denominations. They have so sinned against their God that he has withdrawn his power. However, they are so far from him that they carry on just as before, unaware that he has departed from them (Revelation 3:17–18).

None so blind

If Shakespeare's words are true of anyone, they are true of Samson:

But love is blind and lovers cannot see
The pretty follies that themselves commit;
For if they could, Cupid himself would blush
To see me thus transformed to a boy.[2]

Samson never seems to question why it is that Delilah is obsessed with knowing the secret of his strength. He is not alerted to danger by the fact that each lie is followed by both an experiment to see if he has spoken the truth and the repeated cry, 'Samson, the Philistines are upon you!' Saddest of all is that it never occurs to Samson to answer the question with the plain and simple truth expressed so eloquently by Moses:

The LORD is my strength and my song;
   he has become my salvation.
He is my God, and I will praise him,
   my father's God, and I will exalt him.
The LORD is a warrior;
   the LORD is his name (Exodus 15:2–3).

Such a declaration of faith would have answered the question, ended the nagging and terrified the Philistines just as the account of God's exploits had terrified the inhabitants of Jericho before them (Joshua 2).

The person of Christ

Samson's besetting sin was his inappropriate love for women. Ours may be similar or something quite different. We need to be aware that all sin is *sin* and incurs the wrath of God (Romans 1:18; 2:5–11). Paul occasionally used a literary device known as juxtaposition, a fancy way of saying that he placed certain things next to each other, for example in a list, for emphasis and effect. We see this in Paul's second letter to the Corinthians, where 'gossip' and 'sexual sin and debauchery' are both concerns of his within the life of the church (12:20–21). Another example is seen in Galatians: 'The acts of the sinful nature are obvious: sexual immorality, impurity and debauchery; idolatry and witchcraft; hatred, discord, jealousy, fits of rage, selfish ambition, dissensions, factions and envy; drunkenness, orgies, and the like. I warn you, as I did before, that those who live like this will not inherit the kingdom of God' (5:19–21). Here, 'factions' (what we might call cliques) finds itself in close proximity to 'witchcraft' and 'orgies'. The point I am seeking to make is that no sin can be regarded lightly. There is no place for us to condemn others and condone ourselves simply on the grounds that the symptoms we are manifesting are different. The disease is the same: SIN.

Jesus alone is without sin, a fact to which Scripture testifies again and again. Consider the contrast between these two verses: 'For we do not have a high priest who is unable to sympathize with our weaknesses, but we have one who has been tempted in every way, just as we are—yet was without sin' (Hebrews 4:15—referring to the Lord Jesus); and 'If we claim to be without sin, we deceive ourselves and the truth is not in us' (1 John 1:8—referring to believers). It therefore follows that Christ's dealings with women, like the rest of his life, were beyond reproach. An interesting example is the incident of the woman caught in adultery recorded in John 7:53–8:11.³ In that encounter Jesus made a number of extremely pertinent points:

- 'If any one of you is without sin, let him be the first to throw a stone at her'—thus exposing the hypocrisy of the Pharisees;
- 'neither do I condemn you'—asserting his own right to either condemn or acquit, a prerogative belonging solely to God. In so claiming he was, of course, also affirming his own sinlessness;
- 'Go now and leave your life of sin'—making it clear that the purpose of his mercy was not to endorse her lifestyle but provide an opportunity for repentance and a renewed life.

The hymn writer Charitie Lees De Chenez (1841–1923) penned these great verses in her marvellous hymn *Before the throne of God* above:

Because the sinless Saviour died,
My sinful soul is counted free;
For God the Just is satisfied
To look on him, and pardon me.

Behold him there! the risen Lamb!
My perfect, spotless righteousness,
The great unchangeable I AM,
The King of glory and of grace!⁴

Both verses rightly stress the link between Christ's sinlessness and our salvation. It is only because, as a man, he lived a perfect life that the offering he made of himself on the cross could possibly atone for our sins. Had he sinned, death would have been rightly claiming its prize. It was only because He was God that his life had the infinite value needed to pay the price for the sins of all his people. Justification, what Philip Eveson calls 'The Great Exchange',[5] is that transaction of grace when Christ takes upon himself our sins and imputes to us his righteousness.

The Bible uses marriage as an illustration of the relationship that God wants with his people. It should be one of exclusive faithfulness. It is striking that Christ calls his church his 'bride' and that God uses the picture of adultery to express his pain when we sin.

Questions

COMPARING SCRIPTURE WITH SCRIPTURE

1. What is the extent and nature of human sin? See Romans 1:18–32 and 1 John 1:5–2:2.

2. What does the Bible teach about sex and marriage? See Genesis 2:18–24; Matthew 19:4–5; Ephesians 5:22–33; Colossians 3:18–19; 1 Peter 3:1–7; and Proverbs 5:15–23.

3. Consider some of the passages where marriage is used as a picture of the relationship between God and his people—Ezekiel 23:36–39; Hosea 2:1–13; Ephesians 5:22–33; and Revelation 19:6–8. What do we learn from them?

APPLYING SCRIPTURE TO DAILY LIFE

1. Why does it matter so much that Christ was without sin? What should be our response to this truth?

2. Does the present trend away from marriage and towards living together matter?

3. Is it true that sinful choices always have consequences? Think about your own personal experience.

FOR PERSONAL APPLICATION

I have added a third section of questions for this chapter, intended *solely for personal reflection*. The nature of the questions makes them inappropriate for discussion but very valuable for personal, prayerful self-examination. I offer them because of the truly frightening statistics relating to the access of online pornography and the escalating divorce rate. It would seem that both are endemic, even among Christians. Some of the Scriptures below are slanted towards men but the principles are easily adapted by women, who are not immune from the same temptations.

1. Samson's sins were sexual in nature, especially in the light of the high standard set by the Lord Jesus Christ in Matthew 5:28. How free from that sin are you?

2. Consider the advice given in Proverbs 6:20–29. What defence mechanisms are there here for the believer?

3. Consider both the encouragement and the warnings in Proverbs 5:15–23.

Notes

1 http://en.wikipedia.org/wiki/Samson_and_Delilah_(1996_film) [accessed 10 August 2006].

2 **William Shakespeare** (1564–1616), *The Merchant of Venice*, Act II, Scene 6.

3 The earliest MSS do not include this passage and it is omitted or consigned to a footnote in many modern translations including the NIV and ESV. Despite the controversy surrounding the inclusion of this passage in the Gospel of John, the eminent scholar and preacher D. A. Carson is surely right when he says that 'there is little reason for doubting that the event here described occurred, even if in its written form it did not in the beginning belong to the canonical books' (**Carson,** *The Gospel According to John*, p. 333).

4 *Christian Hymns* 258 and elsewhere.

5 **P. Eveson,** *The Great Exchange* (Leominster: Day One Publications, 2004).

Death in Gaza

The fate to which the Philistines subjected Samson was both cruel and common. First his eyes were gouged out, and then he was shackled with bronze fetters before being removed to Gaza where he was forced to grind corn like a dumb ox. This punishment might seem unbelievably cruel to us but as we can see from 2 Kings 25:7, the same thing was done to King Zedekiah. It was designed to render the prisoner helpless and therefore no further threat, and also to humiliate him and his people, and act as a salutary warning to any others who might consider rebellion.

So we come to the final and, in some ways, the most significant act of this breathtaking drama, the death of Samson. If the narrative stopped at 16:21 it would be a tragedy of epic proportions:

- Israel is still in bondage to the Philistines;
- Her judge is now a pathetic, enfeebled creature;
- Guile has triumphed over even God-given strength.

There is a well-known saying, possibly derived from the frequent appearance of a well-built soprano at the end of an opera, 'It's not over until the fat lady sings'—indicating that until the final curtain has dropped the plot is not yet finished.[1] This is certainly true of the Samson story. The purposes of God are not to be thwarted by a scheming woman, a cruel nation or even his deeply damaged servant. They will come to fruition; they must do so because, after all, he is God. Jeremiah said, 'The LORD's purposes against Babylon stand' (Jeremiah 51:29); so, too, do his purposes against Philistia. The psalmist wisely observes:

The LORD foils the plans of the nations;
he thwarts the purposes of the peoples.
But the plans of the LORD stand firm for ever,
the purposes of his heart through all generations (Psalm 33:10–11).

Samson, however, has no monopoly on foolishness. The Philistines, elated with their victory over Israel's judge, grow complacent. They now see Samson as a pathetic, blind prisoner, fit only for their sport. They forget the link between his hair and his strength, and fail to notice that the period of captivity has restored the one; a plea to God's mercy and justice will restore the other. Samson knows that the days of his effective service for God are at an end. To a large measure he has failed over the past twenty years to fulfil his potential and deliver Israel. He now, belatedly, sets his calling before his personal survival. He seeks a final endowment of strength which he will use to maximum effect. He has no intention of wasting his strength on a conflict with his guards; instead he forms a 'grand plan': the destruction of the temple of a false God and a greater slaughter of his enemies than he has achieved in a lifetime. Perhaps this is true wisdom at last.

The purpose of the Philistine celebration was twofold: they wished to make sacrifice to their god Dagon (meaning 'little fish' and represented by a strange idol with the body of a fish but the head and hands of a man[2]) and to celebrate his imagined victory over Samson's God. In this endeavour they succeed in adding blasphemy to idolatry. They repeatedly give glory to a dead image and withhold it from the living God. This is always a dangerous practice. Israel was solemnly warned: 'For the LORD your God is a consuming fire, a jealous God' (Deuteronomy 4:24). Indeed, 'Jealous' is one of the names by which God reveals himself (Exodus 34:14).

The Philistines entertain themselves by making sport of their humbled enemy; this, it seems, goes on until, wearied by 'performing' for them, Samson begs respite from his captors and rests beside the pillars that support the temple structure. Above him are 3,000 of his tormentors crowding the roof of the building and enjoying their day's cruel entertainment. With simple dignity the narrator informs us of the single act that transformed victory into disaster for the Philistines and tragedy into triumph for Samson—Samson prayed.

What a power there is in prayer:

- Abraham prays and Abimelech and his family are healed (Genesis 20:17);
- Moses prays and plagues descend on the land of Egypt (Exodus 8:30);
- David prays and the hand of God's judgement is stayed (2 Samuel 24:25);
- Peter prays and Tabitha is restored to life (Acts 9:40).

Little wonder that Paul encourages us in one of the most succinct verses in Scripture: 'Pray continually' (1 Thessalonians 5:17).

On this occasion Samson honours his God in a way we have not seen in him before. His calling God 'Sovereign LORD' (NIV), or 'Lord GOD', as many of the other translations render it, places him in the company of Abram (Genesis 15:2, 8), Joshua (Joshua 7:7), Gideon (Judges 6:22), David (2 Samuel 7:18–29), Isaiah (Isaiah 30:15), Jeremiah (Jeremiah 4:10), Ezekiel (Ezekiel 4:14) and many others including the infant church in Acts 4:24. His petition begins with the simple but fundamental plea 'Remember me'. It is not that Samson thinks God has forgotten him, in the way that you and I might forget an appointment or an anniversary. Rather it is a plea that God will again be active in his life and restore the blessing of his presence. God solemnly warned Israel through Jeremiah that he would *thrust* them from his presence (Jeremiah 7:15). The deepest fear of David was expressed in this way: 'Do not cast me from your presence or take your Holy Spirit from me' (Psalm 51:11)—this was the nightmare in which Samson now lived. His darkness at this moment was far more than that which he suffered in consequence of his blindness. In some small measure he was experiencing a foretaste of hell, the hell which the Lord Jesus described in these terrifying terms: '… the darkness, where there will be weeping and gnashing of teeth' (Matthew 25:30).

Samson knew himself to be such a worthless servant and was weary of drinking that bitter cup. Samson was not, however, in hell; there is no escape from hell. He was in what men sometimes refer to, wrongly, as a 'living hell'. Mercifully for him there was still hope. Unlike the rich man in Jesus' sobering tale there was not yet a permanent gulf fixed between him and his God (Luke 16:19–31). His prayer is mirrored by the supplication of Jeremiah:

You understand, O LORD;
   remember me and care for me.
   Avenge me on my persecutors.
You are long-suffering—do not take me away;
   think of how I suffer reproach for your sake (Jeremiah 15:15).

His plea is for one last endowment of strength to avenge his lost sight and destroy his and Israel's enemies. It is a plea God grants in spectacular manner. There is also a simple postscript: 'Let me die with the Philistines.' No miracle of healing the blind was to take place until the advent of the ministry of Jesus. If Samson were to live, his usefulness would be over and he would remain a sad spectacle. It is important to note that Samson does not commit suicide. He leaves the question of his life and death in the hands of God, whose prerogative it is to both give and take away.

The prayer is answered and the epitaph written. Mercifully it is not, as it might well have been: 'He failed in his task.' Rather it is: 'He killed many more when he died than while he lived.' It is surely on account of this one mighty act that he gains inclusion in the Hebrews 11 list of the notable men and women of faith.

The person of Christ

Samson stands out as a man lacking in wisdom; however, it is recorded of the Lord Jesus Christ that: 'The child grew and became strong; he was filled with wisdom, and the grace of God was upon him' (Luke 2:40).

That fullness of wisdom never departed from him. In Samson we see a failure to grasp the true nature of those around him; in Christ we see the exact opposite. Nathanael's amazement is well-justified (John 1:48), as is John's comment: 'He did not need man's testimony about man, for he knew what was in a man' (John 2:25).

Christ's wisdom is evidenced in many familiar passages; a good example was his turning the tables on the Pharisees when they sought to trap him with a trick question on paying taxes to the Roman oppressors; his answer, 'Give to Caesar what is Caesar's, and to God what is God's' (Matthew 22:21), has become an enduring maxim to guide God's people in the conflicting allegiances they sometimes face. Christ was not taken in by the self-deceptive confidence of Peter that asked: 'Lord, why can't I follow you now? I will lay down my life for you' (John 13:37). Instead he predicted a spectacular fall from grace, but assured the errant disciple of comfort and restoration, and revealed to him the secret of future fruitfulness (John 15).

In his grace (Ephesians 1:7–8) that wisdom is also pledged to those who become his disciples: 'For I will give you words and wisdom that none of your adversaries will be able to resist or contradict' (Luke 21:15). In an extended passage on wisdom (1 Corinthians 1:18–3:19) the Apostle Paul contrasts 'the wisdom of the wise' (1 Corinthians 1:19) with 'God's secret wisdom' (1 Corinthians 2:7). The world seeks after the former, but the gospel is preached in the power of the latter.

The life of Samson would seem, without these final eight verses, to end on a note of tragedy. A foreshortened life of Jesus might, at first glance, appear to do the same. Certainly the reasons would be quite different. Most people are prepared to concede to Jesus the accolade 'a good man', even if they wish to deny him the glory due to him as the God-man. There is, however, a persistent tendency with some to paint him as a tragic figure: the good man rejected by the wicked world, betrayed by his friend but nevertheless offering an example of nobility in the face of defeat. What a travesty that picture is! It is wrong for two fundamental reasons.

Firstly, Jesus was never the helpless victim of circumstances. His death was predicted well before his birth (Isaiah 53 and Psalm 22 are good examples). It was also a constant theme of Christ's own ministry (Matthew 16:21; 17:12; and John 13:33). Caiaphas gave the following evil advice: 'You do not realize that it is better for you that one man die for the people than that the whole nation perish' (John 11:50), on which John comments, 'He did not say this on his own, but as high priest that year he prophesied that Jesus would die for the Jewish nation' (v. 51).

There is ample evidence in the Gospel accounts of Jesus's last days that he was fully aware and fully in control. He knew that Judas would betray him and could easily have taken evasive action (John 13:21). In the account of his trial before Pilate we are sometimes left wondering who the judge is and who the prisoner (Matthew 27:11–26). Even on the cross he was in control, a truth eloquently attested to by John (John 19:30) and in keeping with Christ's own prediction: 'The reason my Father loves me is that I lay down my life—only to take it up again. No one takes it from me, but I lay it down of my own accord. I have authority to lay it down and authority to take it up again. This command I received from my Father' (John 10:17–18).

Secondly, the death of Jesus was not the end of the story: the 'fat lady' still has not sung. The enduring picture of Jesus is not of a corpse suspended on a crucifix, it is of the glorious, risen, ascended Lord. Paul draws our attention to the centrality of the resurrection when he reminds us: 'If only for this life we have hope in Christ, we are to be pitied more than all men. But Christ has indeed been raised from the dead, the firstfruits of those who have fallen asleep. For since death came through a man, the resurrection of the dead comes also through a man (1 Corinthians 15:19–21).

Jesus, like Samson, succeeded in achieving more in his death than he did in his life. His life was replete with incidents of healing, deliverance and raising the dead; how, one might ask, could all that be surpassed? The answer lies partly in the relative importance of time and eternity. All the miracles of healing and the raising of the dead cannot obscure the fact that death still eventually claimed its prey. Lazarus succumbed to its clutches a second time; he was again laid to rest in his tomb and the grave was destined to be the resting place of all those Jesus had healed. They may have died having seen, heard and leapt for joy, but they all died. The following general statement, 'Just as man is destined to die once, and after that to face judgement …' (Hebrews 9:27), permits no exceptions. What was accomplished in his death, in contrast, echoes through eternity. Creation lets out a triumphant shout of unrestrained joy.

When the perishable has been clothed with the imperishable, and the mortal with immortality, then the saying that is written will come true: 'Death has been swallowed up in victory.'

'Where, O death, is your victory?

Where, O death, is your sting?'

The sting of death is sin, and the power of sin is the law. But thanks be to God! He gives us the victory through our Lord Jesus Christ (1 Corinthians 15:54–57).

In his death Christ, who by his perfect life had satisfied the just demands of the law, defeated death by breaking the power of sin. The resurrection was the evidence that the offering Christ made was acceptable to the Father; the new and living way was opened up (Hebrews 10:19–22) for men and women to find peace (Romans 5:1–2) and reconciliation (2 Corinthians 5:17–21) with God.

Questions

COMPARING SCRIPTURE WITH SCRIPTURE

1. What does Luke mean when he says of Jesus that 'the child grew and became strong; he was filled with wisdom, and the grace of God was upon him' (2:40)? In what sense could the God-man Christ Jesus grow?

2. Read 1 Corinthians 1:18–3:19. What difference do you see there between the wisdom of the world and that of God?

3. What can we learn from a comparison of the death of Samson (Judges 16:23–31) and that of Christ (Matthew 27:45–56; Luke 23:26–49; and John 19:1–37)?

APPLYING SCRIPTURE TO DAILY LIFE

1. What practical steps can we take to ensure that we learn the appropriate lessons from the experiences of life?

2. How can we obtain wisdom and knowledge? (See Proverbs 2:6; 9:10; Ecclesiastes 2:26; Isaiah 33:4–5; 1 Corinthians 12:8; Colossians 1:9–10; 2:2–3.)

3. How would you like people to remember you at the end of your life?

Notes

1 http://www.worldwidewords.org/qa/qa-ita1.htm [accessed 16 August 2006].
2 **M. Easton,** *Easton's Bible Dictionary* (Oak Harbor, WA: Logos Research Systems, 1996).

Samson and providence

Having followed the life of Samson through from conception to death, there are two aspects of his life that we will consider before we end this study. The first is providence and the second, prayer.

One of the most significant features of the Samson story is the added light it throws on the important subject of God's providence.[1] Elwell helpfully defines it in this way: 'Providence occurs because God cares about the universe and everyone in it. ... God visits, touches, communicates, controls, and intervenes, coming before and between man and his needs. Providence is ground for thankfulness.'[2]

Providence is evident in the lives of many biblical characters, notably Joseph (Genesis 37–50), Moses (the book of Exodus), Ruth (the book of Ruth), David (1 Samuel 16–1 Kings 2:12), Ezra (the book of Ezra), Nehemiah (the book of Nehemiah) and Esther (the book of Esther). It is not to be equated with fate, which is the supposed operation of unalterable forces, nor is it the same as luck, which is perceived to be entirely impersonal. It is the hand of God in history, and it is a key element in Samson's life.

Let's examine the elements of providence that we see in these few chapters of Judges.

1. It begins in chapter 13 where we see, once again, that the response of God to the sin of his people is mercy. This has been evidenced already in the book through the raising up of such characters as Deborah, Barak, Gideon and Jephthah. The ultimate expression of this mercy is always the raising up of a deliverer: Joseph from the Egyptian famine; Moses from slavery in Egypt; Esther to save the people from the hand of Haman and annihilation; and supremely Christ to deliver from sin, Satan and death.

2. God is in no hurry; he always has a long-term strategy. Joseph had many trials to face before rising to Pharaoh's right hand; Moses had eighty years of preparation for forty of ministry. So our story begins nine months before the birth of Samson, and presumably twenty or thirty years before he first confronts the Philistines.

3. God's plans are secret until he chooses to reveal them, and then they

are often revealed progressively. So in 14:4, as we have noted, 'His [Samson's] parents did not know that this was from the LORD, who was seeking an occasion to confront the Philistines; for at that time they were ruling over Israel.'

4. God's methods are often startling. Slavery and prison were the stepping stones to power for Joseph; murder, exile and forty years as a shepherd were the preparation for Moses; bereavement, a queen's disgrace and success in a beauty contest were the route to influence for Esther and the consequent salvation of the Jews. In that light, a petty family quarrel becoming the catalyst for the start of war with the Philistines seems less surprising.

5. God's choice of such a flawed man as Samson also has lessons to teach us. Service to God, like salvation, is not on the basis of merit but grace. David was a profoundly flawed man yet is described in these terms: 'The LORD has sought out a man after his own heart and appointed him leader of his people' (1 Samuel 13:14). Paul explains it in this way: 'But we have this treasure in jars of clay to show that this all-surpassing power is from God and not from us' (2 Corinthians 4:7).

The tantalizing thought throughout the story is this—what might Samson have achieved if his heart had been wholly set on God? The tragedy is that, because he didn't fulfil his potential, he only began 'the deliverance of Israel from the hands of the Philistines' (13:5); he would never complete it. The Philistines would remain a thorn in the side of Israel until the days of David. In this, Samson is a picture of Israel the nation:

- Called by God;
- Often disobedient;
- Often sinning;
- Sometimes seemingly unaware of his calling;
- Selfish, immoral and egotistic;
- Suffering the just consequences of sin;
- Nevertheless fulfilling, at least in part, the purposes of God;
- A picture of the triumph of grace.

6. The providence of God is seen in the incident of the lion's attack. The event serves two significant purposes. Firstly, it is the first occasion on which the Spirit of God comes upon Samson and it serves to prepare him

for what is to come. Soon he must perform super-human feats of strength in opposition to his enemies—and they can only be accomplished through the Spirit of God. Just as Gideon had to rely on God, not on his 32,000-strong army (even though the Midianites were as thick as locusts on the ground (Judges 7)), so Samson will have to rely on the Lord. The maxim of the people of God must always be: 'Some trust in chariots and some in horses, but we trust in the name of the LORD our God' (Psalm 20:7); their warning must be:

Woe to those who go down to Egypt for help,
    who rely on horses,
who trust in the multitude of their chariots
    and in the great strength of their horsemen,
but do not look to the Holy One of Israel,
    or seek help from the LORD (Isaiah 31:1).

Secondly, this event will provide Samson with the riddle that he sets before the wedding companions, which through their cheating and his wife's betrayal sets off the first wave of conflict.

7. The final and, arguably, greatest providence occurs in chapter 16. The Lord ensures that the Philistines choose Gaza, site of Samson's infidelity with the prostitute and a previous deliverance (16:1–3) to be the scene of his final humiliation. Having already blinded and humiliated him, their lust for vengeance is not satisfied and they make a fatal mistake. They will torment Israel's judge in the temple of their god Dagon, and in so doing demonstrate the victory of the Philistines over him and of their god over his God.

Later, in the days of Samuel, God permitted the Ark of the Covenant to fall into the hands of another generation of this same people (2 Samuel 4–6). He did so in order to punish Israel and break their tragic complacency, but the Philistines again foolishly took it as Dagon's victory over the true God. Having set the Ark before their idol, they returned to find his image prostrate before the symbol of the presence of the Lord. This act of pride brought down on their heads a great plague and resulted in them returning the Ark to their enemies.

Charles Spurgeon once said that 'providence is nothing more than goodness in action';[3] the goodness of God is certainly seen in the life of Samson.

The person of Christ

Let's look again at some of these aspects of providence as they relate to the person of Christ.

Mercy was one of Christ's most precious characteristics. In Matthew's Gospel alone we read specifically that it was extended: to the Canaanite woman whose daughter was demon-possessed (15:21–28); to a boy enduring the same affliction (17:14–19); and to two blind men (20:29–34). The same author records it as an important part of Christ's teaching (5:7; 9:13; 12:7;13:44–45; 18:21–35; and 23:23). It is key to Paul's personal understanding of God's gracious dealings with himself: 'But for that very reason I was shown mercy so that in me, the worst of sinners, Christ Jesus might display his unlimited patience as an example for those who would believe on him and receive eternal life' (1 Timothy 1:16).

Along with grace and peace, mercy is also a familiar component of New Testament benedictions (1 Timothy 1:2; 2 Timothy 1:2; and 2 John 3). It is with confidence that we can heed the encouragement of Jude: 'Keep yourselves in God's love as you wait for the mercy of our Lord Jesus Christ to bring you to eternal life' (Jude 21).

God is in no hurry. The first promise of Christ as redeemer came as part of the story of the fall of man in Genesis 3. Slowly, over many generations the promise was elaborated and reinforced until finally John the Baptist had the immense privilege of proclaiming that the waiting was over and that the one who would 'take away the sin of the world' (John 1:29) had come. Jesus spent some thirty years in silent preparation for three brief years of public ministry, and 2,000 years have now passed in waiting for his return in glory to usher in the fullness of the long-awaited kingdom. We do well to heed Peter's reminder: 'But do not forget this one thing, dear friends: With the Lord a day is like a thousand years, and a thousand years are like a day. The Lord is not slow in keeping his promise, as some understand slowness. He is patient with you, not wanting anyone to perish, but everyone to come to repentance' (2 Peter 3:8–9).

God's plans are secret until he reveals them. Despite the clear announcement by John referred to above there was a mystery surrounding the person and work of Christ that was only slowly unveiled in the Gospels. So when Peter made his momentous declaration that Jesus is 'the Christ, the Son of the living God', it was hailed as not having been revealed to him by man, but by Christ's Father in heaven (Matthew 16:16–17). Still the journey was not over; Jesus had so much still to say to the disciples that John needed five chapters (13–17) to record it for us. Still the disciples on the Emmaus Road needed further instruction, so '… beginning with Moses and all the Prophets, [Jesus] explained to them what was said in all the Scriptures concerning himself' (Luke 24:27).

Luke prefaces the book of Acts by reminding us that his first volume was 'all that Jesus began to do and to teach' (1:1); this second volume would inform us of all that he continued to teach through his disciples by the outpoured Holy Spirit. The New Testament letters continued that divine revelation about Jesus. Even then the revelation was not complete, not until John, a prisoner on the island of Patmos, was 'on the Lord's Day in the Spirit' (Revelation 1:10) and in visions saw 'what must take place after this' (Revelation 4:1).

How foolish we are if we expect to be exceptions to this rule and know what lies in our futures. No! We are called to live 'by faith, not by sight' (2 Corinthians 5:7).

God's methods are often startling. In Old Testament days the enemies of God's people were flesh and blood; this is not so in the church era: now they are principalities and powers (Ephesians 6:12). It took some while for this simple truth to dawn on the disciples. Initially they expected Jesus to act like Samson and the other Old Testament warriors and 'slay his enemies', so that when Jesus was rejected by a Samaritan village, James and John helpfully offered 'to call fire down from heaven to destroy them' (Luke 9:51–55). How wrong they were! As John eventually saw in his vision, although Jesus was indeed the 'Lion of the tribe of Judah, the Root of David', he appeared among men as a lamb to be slain (Revelation 5:5). His method of overcoming evil was with good; he would not slay his enemies but offer himself up to be slain by them. In that way he would achieve what John Owen famously entitled one of his writings, 'The death of death in the death of Christ'.4

Flawed men fulfilled the purposes of God for many of his mighty deeds, but for the work of redemption absolute perfection was essential. Jesus alone could meet this criterion. His life and ministry were divinely affirmed by an audible voice from heaven on several occasions (Matthew 3:17; 17:5); his death was validated by his resurrection in power.

Questions

COMPARING SCRIPTURE WITH SCRIPTURE

1. Was the advice of Gamaliel (Acts 5:34–39) sound? If so, how do we account for the spectacular rise of cults such as the 'Jehovah Witnesses' and religions such as Islam? If it was unsound, how was the providence of God at work in the incident?

2. What are the implications of the providence of God seen in the ministry of Paul? (See Acts 16:6–10.)

APPLYING SCRIPTURE TO DAILY LIFE

1. What comforts can we take from knowledge of the providence of God?

2. In what sense is God's revelation about himself complete? Does this mean we know all there is to know about him?

Notes

1 See also the author's book *Exploring Esther.*

2 **W. A. Elwell** and **B. J. Beitzel,** *Baker Encyclopedia of the Bible* (Grand Rapids, MI: Baker Book House, 1988).

3 **C. H. Spurgeon,** *Morning and Evening: Daily Readings* (April 9 PM) (Oak Harbor, WA: Logos Research Systems, 1995).

4 John Owen (1616–1683), a Puritan theologian and preacher whose entire works are available from the Banner of Truth Trust, Edinburgh. *The Death of Death*, first published in 1648, was his definitive work on the atonement.

Samson's prayers

The first recorded prayer of Samson

The first of the only two recorded prayers on the lips of Samson comes in chapter 15:

Because he was very thirsty, he cried out to the LORD, 'You have given your servant this great victory. Must I now die of thirst and fall into the hands of the uncircumcised?' Then God opened up the hollow place in Lehi, and water came out of it. When Samson drank, his strength returned and he revived. So the spring was called En Hakkore, and it is still there in Lehi (vv. 18–19).

This prayer follows his great victory over the Philistines when he slays 1,000 of them with the fresh jawbone of an ass. Between the victory and the prayer comes this poem or song of triumph on Samson's lips as recorded in verse 16:

With a donkey's jawbone
    I have made donkeys of them.
With a donkey's jawbone
    I have killed a thousand men.

It is here we must start if we are rightly to evaluate the prayer. The poem is another glimpse of the unexpected literary genius of Samson; the Hebrew demonstrates a complex structure with both parallelism and wordplay.[1] The Hebrew words for 'donkey' and 'heap' are spelt the same: *ḥᵃmôr*. Even more significant is the contrast between this poem and Deborah's song in Judges 5. Both judges have been enabled by God to win great victories, both mark the occasion poetically and both recount the victory, but there the comparison ends. Deborah's song, admittedly much longer than Samson's, is full of God. She mentions the Lord thirteen times, exhorts the people to 'Praise the Lord' twice (vv. 2,9), and acknowledges in very clear terms that the victory was from the hands of God and him alone. In Samson's poem it is 'I have …'.

As we turn to the prayer, sadly this same egocentric trait is in evidence. The first recorded prayer on the lips of Israel's judge is for himself. He does, admittedly, begin by ascribing, somewhat belatedly, the victory to God but then launches into a thinly disguised recrimination—'Must I now die of thirst and fall into the hands of the uncircumcised?' The tone of praise, trust and submission we are familiar with from other great prayers in the Old Testament appears to be absent. Compare these few sample prayers with that of Samson.

JACOB'S PRAYER BEFORE CROSSING THE JORDAN TO MEET ESAU

Then Jacob prayed, 'O God of my father Abraham, God of my father Isaac, O LORD, who said to me, "Go back to your country and your relatives, and I will make you prosper", I am unworthy of all the kindness and faithfulness you have shown your servant. I had only my staff when I crossed this Jordan, but now I have become two groups. Save me, I pray, from the hand of my brother Esau, for I am afraid he will come and attack me, and also the mothers with their children. But you have said, "I will surely make you prosper and will make your descendants like the sand of the sea, which cannot be counted"' (Genesis 32:9–12).

MOSES' PRAYER FOR ISRAEL

I prayed to the LORD and said, 'O Sovereign LORD, do not destroy your people, your own inheritance that you redeemed by your great power and brought out of Egypt with a mighty hand. Remember your servants Abraham, Isaac and Jacob. Overlook the stubbornness of this people, their wickedness and their sin. Otherwise, the country from which you brought us will say, "Because the LORD was not able to take them into the land he had promised them, and because he hated them, he brought them out to put them to death in the desert." But they are your people, your inheritance that you brought out by your great power and your outstretched arm' (Deuteronomy 9:26–29).

HANNAH'S PRAYER IN HER BARRENNESS.

In bitterness of soul Hannah wept much and prayed to the LORD. And she made a vow, saying, 'O LORD Almighty, if you will only look upon your servant's misery and remember me, and not forget your servant but give her a son, then I will give him to the LORD for all the days of his life, and no razor will ever be used on his head' (1 Samuel 1:10–11).

ELIJAH ON MOUNT CARMEL

At the time of sacrifice, the prophet Elijah stepped forward and prayed: 'O LORD, God of Abraham, Isaac and Israel, let it be known today that you are God in Israel and that I am your servant and have done all these things at your command. Answer me, O LORD, answer me, so these people will know that you, O LORD, are God, and that you are turning their hearts back again' (1 Kings 18:36–37).

Even Samson's father's prayer has more to commend it: 'Then Manoah prayed to the LORD: "O Lord, I beg you, let the man of God you sent to us come again to teach us how to bring up the boy who is to be born"' (Judges 13:8).

The last recorded prayer of Samson

The only other recorded prayer of Samson comes at the bitter end of his life. Blind and humiliated, he now seeks the face of his God for the last time. 'Then Samson prayed to the LORD, "O Sovereign LORD, remember me. O God, please strengthen me just once more, and let me with one blow get revenge on the Philistines for my two eyes"' (Judges 16:28).

This time there is a note of praise and an ascription of glory in the words 'O Sovereign Lord'. The same words seem to exhibit a clearer understanding of the person and glory of the Lord; he has always been, but now is acknowledged to be, 'Sovereign'. True, there is still a personal element to the prayer: the revenge is sought for 'my two eyes', but there is no note of recrimination. Perhaps Samson had learned at last that the 'wages of sin is death' (Romans 6:23). All he has ever achieved has been by the grace of God; all he has failed to accomplish has been as a result of his own sin. So it is with all of God's people. What he seeks is vengeance but what he acknowledges is that it can only come from the hand of God. In this his plea is a godly one. Vengeance is, and must always remain, the prerogative of the Lord. He alone is wise enough to wield such an awesome weapon. Its use was taken out of man's hands as early as the days of Cain in answer to his lament:

Cain said to the LORD, 'My punishment is more than I can bear. Today you are driving me from the land, and I will be hidden from your presence; I will be a restless wanderer on the earth, and whoever finds me will kill me.' But the LORD said to him, 'Not so; if anyone kills Cain, he will suffer vengeance seven times over.' Then the LORD put a mark on Cain so that no one who found him would kill him (Genesis 4:13–15).

From that day onwards it has been in the exclusive domain of God. As Paul wisely reminds us, 'Do not take revenge, my friends, but leave room for God's wrath, for it is written: "It is mine to avenge; I will repay," says the Lord' (Romans 12:19).

In the Old Testament God caused 'cities of refuge' to be established so that men would have somewhere to flee from the retribution of those seeking personal vengeance (Numbers 35:9–15). Christ commands his people to follow a far different path: 'You have heard that it was said, "Love your neighbour and hate your enemy." But I tell you: Love your enemies and pray for those who persecute you' (Matthew 5:43–44).

The person of Christ

While there are only two recorded prayers on the lips of Samson, the account of Christ's life is replete with them. Prayer was an integral part of his walk with God. Luke sums it up well in the simple statement: 'But Jesus often withdrew to lonely places and prayed' (Luke 5:16).

Prayer marked out the significant moments in Jesus' public ministry: he spent the whole night in prayer before choosing his disciples (Luke 6:12–16), and it was after a time of personal prayer that he asked the question, 'Who do the crowds say I am?' then 'But what about you? … Who do you say I am?', making way for Peter's great confession of faith: 'The Christ of God.'

The only personal request from the Saviour to his disciples was made on the night before his death, and was simply that they stayed with him while he prayed to the Father (Matthew 26:36–46). The fullest example we have of his prayer is recorded in John 17. It is this passage rather than Matthew 6:9–13 that we should call 'The Lord's Prayer'; that prayer is really 'The Disciples' Prayer'.

In John 17 we see Jesus praying for:
• his own and the Father's glory (vv. 1–6);
• the protection of his disciples through the power of his name (v. 11);
• their unity (v. 11);

- a full measure of joy for them (v. 13);
- their protection from 'the evil one' (v. 15);
- their sanctification through God's word of truth (v. 17);
- those who would come to faith through the first disciples' testimony (v. 20);
- for them all to be with him (v. 24);
- for them to see his glory (v. 24);
- that God's love might be in them (v. 26);
- that he himself might be in them (v. 26).

This is truly prayer at its most sublime.

Questions

COMPARING SCRIPTURE WITH SCRIPTURE

1. What lessons can we learn from the intercession of Abraham in Genesis 18:16–33?

2. Consider the great prayers of Paul in Ephesians 1:2–14; 1:15–21; 3:14–21; and 6:19–20.

3. What are the limitations, if any, to the promise of Jesus in Matthew 21:22?

APPLYING SCRIPTURE TO DAILY LIFE

1. What practical steps can we take to improve our own prayer times?

2. How could 'The Disciples' Prayer' (Matthew 6:9–13) help our own prayer lives?[2]

3. What are the different elements to prayer? Think, for example, of intercession, praise, thanksgiving, etc. How balanced are these elements in your prayer life?

Notes

1 See **Kim,** *The Structure of the Samson Cycle,* for a very detailed and technical analysis of the structure of the Samson story.

2 See **Derek Prime's** marvellous book, *The Lord's Prayer for Today* (Bromley: Day One Publications, 1996).

Samson: hero or villain?

W e have come to the end of the account in Judges of the life of Samson. There is, however, one more passage we must consider:

And what more shall I say? I do not have time to tell about Gideon, Barak, Samson, Jephthah, David, Samuel and the prophets, who through faith conquered kingdoms, administered justice, and gained what was promised; who shut the mouths of lions, quenched the fury of the flames, and escaped the edge of the sword; whose weakness was turned to strength; and who became powerful in battle and routed foreign armies (Hebrews 11:32–34).

The author of this New Testament letter, writing by inspiration of God, firmly places Samson among the great men and women of faith recorded in Scripture. The question that faces us is how this assessment accords with the man we have been studying. There are three options (and numerous half-way positions) open to us:
- We can reject the assessment and argue that Samson is no hero but a weak-willed, womanizing failure.
- We can close our eyes to the moral faults in this judge of Israel and hail him as 'man of God' par excellence.
- We can give full weight to all that we have discovered and seek to interpret it through this text.

Options 1 and 2 can both be safely rejected. Neither is acceptable as neither treats the text of Scripture with the respect it demands. Option 1 renders Hebrews 11:32 a flawed judgement, something we will reject out of hand if our doctrine of the inspiration and infallibility of Scripture is a truly biblical one. Option 2 makes the fatal mistake of equating 'faith' with 'morality'. In reality, we know that men and women of faith are not immune from moral failure. This can be easily demonstrated from the great 'heroes of faith' that precede Samson in Hebrews 11 itself. Three examples will suffice:
- *Noah's* life is marred by his drunkenness that in turn occasioned Ham's sin (Genesis 9:18–29);

- *Abraham* lied twice about the extent of his true relationship with his wife Sarah (Genesis 12:10–20; 20:1–13);
- *Moses* failed to trust the Lord wholeheartedly and so forfeited his right to lead the people of Israel into the promised land (Numbers 20:6–12; Deuteronomy 1:37; 32:48–52).

It is important for us to understand that *faith* and *moral purity* are requirements of God upon his people, but that they are not the same thing. John MacArthur expresses the contrast well when he says:

Samson is not most remembered for his faith, but for his physical strength and personal gullibility. In many ways he was immature and self-centred, unable to cope with the miraculous power God had given him. Yet he was a man of faith. He never doubted that God was the source of his power, of which his hair was only a symbol.[1]

Without faith, we are told, it is impossible for us to please God (Hebrews 11:6). Without purity (or holiness), we are reminded, no one can see God (Hebrews 12:14).

In our evaluation of Samson we could easily dwell on his failings, which in all truth are as spectacular and memorable as his feats of strength. Yet Samson displayed unshakable faith in Israel's God when he prayed for strength to mete out justice to his enemies. God heard his prayer.[2]

God is, however, infinitely gracious, and his last word on his erring servant is a positive one. His mercy ensures that Samson's lasting legacy is to be remembered as a man of faith not a slave of passion. It is his strength not his weakness that is the abiding impression. This 'overlooking' grace of God is a great comfort to all of us who stumblingly seek to follow our God. What inexpressible joy to know that our 'sins and lawless acts [he] will remember no more' (Hebrews 10:17)! They are, of course, only overlooked in the sense that they are not held against us. That, it must be remembered, is only possible because Christ paid a full and sufficient penalty on the cross. Our forgiveness is the fruit of his suffering.

There are numerous lessons for us to learn from the life of Samson:
- about sin and its ever-present challenge to our walk with God;
- about not allowing our strengths to blind us to our weaknesses;

- about wisdom in choosing our companions and the dangers of ungodly company;
- about the foolishness of presumptive arrogance;
- about harsh providences still being part of the grace and mercy of God;
- about the faithfulness of God in the face of our failure.

Perhaps the most poignant lesson concerns 'lost opportunity'—the 'what if?' of Samson the judge. Who knows what potential was wasted by Samson through his self-indulgent lifestyle? What might he have achieved, under God, if he had served with his whole heart?

He acts as a kind of metaphor. Israel, like Samson, was endowed with such amazing gifts and unique calling yet never reached her full potential. Churches and individual believers often tread a similar path of partial obedience. Meditating on what might have been is a fruitless and depressing activity unless it takes us to prayer. The past we can cast upon God's mercy while praying that whatever is left to us of the future might be, as in Samson's case, fully realized in triumphant faith.

Our God is the God of second chances. He graciously called disobedient Jonah a second time to his prophetic task (Jonah 3:1). John Mark, having deserted Paul and Barnabas in Pamphylia, became the cause of a sharp disagreement and temporary separation between the two. Big-hearted Barnabas wanted to give the young man an opportunity to redeem himself but Paul refused (Acts 15:36–41). In this matter Barnabas seems to have been in the right: Mark proved himself to such a great extent that he was later described by the once-reluctant Paul as 'helpful to me in my ministry' (2 Timothy 4:11) and 'my fellow worker' (Philemon 24).

While we live, it is never too late with God. As long as we still breathe we may call on Christ for salvation as did the dying thief (Luke 23:39–43). God may yet give us another opportunity to serve him as he did for both Jonah and Samson. These stories are there to encourage us but also to remind us of the sheer tragic waste of missed opportunity. A careful reading of Scripture will deliver us from both complacency and despair. Jimmy Carter, the former President of the United States, once said, 'I hate to see complacency prevail in our lives when it's so directly contrary to the teaching of Christ.'[3]

We serve such a gracious God, who condescends to use such weak and frail men and women to accomplish his purposes. If we learn anything from Samson, let it be that it is never too late to love and serve him as he so richly deserves. How sad to face our deathbed like Samson, with a last-minute agonized plea for one more chance. How wonderful to have Paul's assurance: 'For I am already being poured out like a drink offering, and the time has come for my departure. I have fought the good fight, I have finished the race, I have kept the faith. Now there is in store for me the crown of righteousness, which the Lord, the righteous Judge, will award to me on that day—and not only to me, but also to all who have longed for his appearing' (2 Timothy 4:6–8).

The person of Christ
In the arrogant lyrics of the song *My Way*, made famous by Frank Sinatra among others, the boast runs:

And now, the end is near;
And so I face the final curtain ...
Regrets, I've had a few;
But then again, too few to mention.

In reality, only one man has ever had reason to approach his death without an unending list of regrets. That man was the God-man, Christ Jesus. His were a perfect infancy, childhood, teenage years and manhood; a life of complete obedience—no opportunity missed, no time wasted, no hasty words later regretted, no lapses of reverence or service, nor sins of omission (things said or done that should not have been), or sins of commission (things not said or done that should have been). He, and he alone, was truly 'without blemish or defect' (1 Peter 1:19). When he prayed outside the tomb of dead Lazarus, he did so with the confidence that his Father always heard and answered him (John 11:41). He had no fear of the approach of Satan, the accuser of God's people, but could say with assurance, 'He has no hold on me' (John 14:30).

The Bible contains the stories of many men and women, exciting stories of daring exploits, tender stories of love, sad stories of loss and grief, tragic stories and happy ones. They all share one thing in common: the main characters and all the minor players were deeply flawed. Some had many admirable traits that warm our hearts; others fill us with loathing. Christ alone causes us to fall upon our knees and cry, 'My Lord and my God' (John 20:28).

Samson may fill us with awe at his strength, impress us with his wit and wisdom, terrify us with his rage, or disgust us with his immorality. We may envy him or pity him, but we could never worship him. Christ possesses a power that is always unleashed for good; his wisdom leaves us speechless with wonder. We may tremble at the thought of his wrath, but we immediately flee to him for our refuge. Instead of envying him, we discover that, in sheer unbounded grace, all that he is and does is on our behalf. There is not a grain of selfishness in the Saviour; he is consumed by a passion for the glory of his Father and the good of his people. Neither can we pity him, for that is an emotion reserved for the helpless. His sufferings in Gethsemane and on the cross were so distinguished by his sovereign choosing as to evoke awe and wonder, but never pity. The contrast serves to remind us that: 'The question is not whether we will die, but how we will live.'4

Questions

COMPARING SCRIPTURE WITH SCRIPTURE

1. Most of the characters in the Bible are portrayed in such a way as to display their faults quite prominently. Joseph in the Old Testament and Barnabas in the New are exceptions. Can you think of others?

2. Consider Ecclesiastes 7:2. If you could have counselled Samson, how would you have applied this verse?

3. Consider 2 Corinthians 7:10. What does Paul say is the difference between 'worldly sorrow' and 'true repentance'? Which did Samson manifest during his lifetime?

APPLYING SCRIPTURE TO DAILY LIFE

1. What would you list among your main spiritual regrets?

2. What practical steps could you take now to be more obedient to God?

3. The mandate to Samson was to 'deliver Israel'. One prominent part of

ours is to 'preach the gospel' (Matthew 28:20). How are we, as individuals and as part of the churches to which we belong, seeking to fulfil that mandate?

Notes

1 **J. MacArthur,** *Hebrews* (Chicago: Moody Press, 1996, p. 365).

2 **S. J. Kistemaker and W. Hendriksen,** *New Testament Commentary: Exposition of Hebrews* (Grand Rapids, MI: Baker Books, 1984).

3 http://education.yahoo.com/reference/quotations/quote/21016;_ylt= Aj56_dbdfrBn.LZU8GqO7mRcCcOF [accessed: 24 January 2007].

4 **Joan Borysenko,** Harvard medical scientist and psychologist, http://www.bellaonline.com/articles/art14723.asp [accessed 25 January 2007].

The Philistines[1]

In our culture, if you call someone a 'philistine' you are implying that he or she is certainly uncultured and probably uncouth. The Merriam-Webster Dictionary defines the term in this way: 'A person who is guided by materialism and is disdainful of intellectual or artistic values'.[2] Such a judgement is a harsh one, reflecting on the character of the people mentioned in Judges. Who, then, were these 'biblical' Philistines?

Their origins

The Philistines were one of the Sea Peoples that appeared at the end of the Late Bronze Age in the south-eastern part of the Mediterranean. Jeremiah (47:4) and Amos (9:7) both state that the Philistines originated in Caphtor. According to Genesis 26:1 they were present in the Negev in patriarchal days, one of their kings, Abimelech, living at Gerar.

Our major source of information concerning them (other than the Bible itself) comes from Egypt. The Egyptians referred to them as mercenaries, calling them Purasti. There is specific reference to them during the reign of Rameses III, who defeated them in a combined land and sea battle towards the beginning of the twelfth century BC. The record of that encounter is preserved in reliefs and inscriptions in the temple at Medinet Habu in Thebes. It was the Philistines and other Sea Peoples, coming supposedly from Greece, the Balkans and even farther north, who migrated south and are believed to have been responsible for the downfall of the Hittite Empire and the destruction of many cities along the coast of Syria and Palestine. Rebuffed by the Egyptian pharaoh Merneptah c.1224–1211, the Philistines began to settle on the Palestinian coastal plain. No written material by the Philistines themselves has so far been discovered.

Their army

The army of the Sea Peoples consisted of three main groups: men, women and children riding in wagons pulled by oxen; infantry; and cavalry. The cavalry consisted of light chariots drawn by two horses, similar to those used by the Egyptians. Each chariot was manned by three soldiers, two armed with two spears each and the third controlling the horses. The infantry was divided into units of four soldiers each. Three of the soldiers were armed with two spears and one straight sword each, the fourth only with a sword. All of them were supplied with round shields and short strap-cuirasses, and wore their distinctive feathered headdresses.

The Philistines carried the images of their gods with them into battle (2 Samuel 5:21). The chief of these was Dagon (Judges 16:23), whose temples were at Mount Gilboa (1 Chronicles 10:10) as well as at Gaza, Ashdod and Beth-Shean.

Their navy
Unlike the Egyptians, who employed galleys, the Philistines favoured single-masted sailing vessels. The prows were suitable for use as battering rams.

Their nation
They appear to have been more of a coalition of city states than a nation in any meaningful sense. Each of their cities was ruled over by a 'lord' (1 Samuel 29:2, NKJV) rather than a king. Most of their personal names, as well as those of their gods, Dagon, Ashtoreth and Baal-Zebub, were Canaanite in origin (Judges 16:23; 1 Samuel 5:2–5; 31:10 and 2 Kings 1:2).

Their involvement with the people of God
- *Genesis 21 and 26:* The Philistines have already a presence in the area and are ruled over by Abimelech.
- *Exodus 13:* The Philistine presence is sufficiently strong for the Lord to cause his people to bypass their territory in case the people are terrified into returning to Egypt.
- *Exodus 23:* Their presence is so established that the western border of the promised land is defined as 'the sea of the Philistines'.
- *Joshua 13:3:* The territory of the Philistines is ruled over by five lords from the cities of Gaza, Ashdod, Ashkelon, Gath and Ekron. They were the principle enemies of the judges Shamgar (Judges 3:31) and Jephthah (Judges 10), as well as Samson.
- *1 Samuel 4 and 5:* A series of battles took place at Aphek and led to over

30,000 deaths among the Israelites. Even more catastrophic, the Ark of the Covenant was captured. The capture, however, had disastrous results for the Philistines and it was eventually returned (ch. 6).

- *1 Samuel 7:* In the early days of Samuel's ministry the people returned to the Lord and put aside their idols. As a result he granted them a great victory at Mizpah. This led to a period of respite from Philistine oppression.
- *1 Samuel 9:16:* The Lord instructs Samuel to anoint Saul the Benjamite as 'leader' over his people specifically to deliver his people from the Philistines, whose oppression had clearly been re-established.
- *1 Samuel 10:5:* They had, by the time of Saul, established numerous garrisons in the land.
- *1 Samuel 13–31:* They were the principle thorn in the side of Saul throughout his time as leader and, later, king. The period included some famous incidents such as the defeat of the giant Goliath by the small lad David (ch. 17) and David's deliverance of Keilah (23:1–6).
- *1 Samuel 27:* During his period fleeing from the anger of King Saul, David hired himself out as a mercenary to the Philistines and lived among them for sixteen months; however, he never raised his sword against his own people.
- *1 Samuel 29:* On the eve of the last major battle between Saul and the Philistines (the battle that resulted in Saul's death), Achish was forced by the other Philistine commanders, who did not trust David, to dispense with his services.
- *2 Samuel 5:* Immediately upon hearing that David had been anointed the new king in Israel, the Philistines marched against him. The Lord granted David victory in successive battles against them.
- *2 Samuel 5:21:* This is of interest as we learn that, on this occasion at least, the Philistines carried their idols into battle with them.
- *2 Samuel 8:1–12:* This lists the Philistines among the nations that David had subdued. Treasure captured from them and others was dedicated to the Lord.
- *2 Samuel 21:15–22:* This makes it clear that the above victory was not a permanent one. It catalogues the remaining battles, including the last battle in which the now aged David was allowed to participate. They

included the killing of the brother of the famous Goliath (see 1 Chronicles 20:5).

- *Isaiah 2:6:* This informs us that the Philistines practised 'divination'.
- *Ezekiel 25:15–17:* This shows that as late as the period of the exile, the ancient antipathy was still there and the Philistines still had some presence in the coastal area.

Notes

1 The main source materials for this appendix were: **A. Negev,** *The Archaeological Encyclopedia of the Holy Land* (3rd ed., New York: Prentice Hall Press, 1996); **Matthews, Chavalas, and Walton,** *The IVP Bible Background Commentary;* Easton, *Easton's Bible Dictionary;* and **Myers,** *The Eerdmans Bible Dictionary.*

2 **Merriam-Webster,** *Merriam-Webster's Collegiate Dictionary* (11th ed., Springfield, MA: Merriam-Webster, 2003).